HERO STATUS

Living Every Day Bolder than Ever

JOE VINETTE

WESTBOW
PRESS®
A DIVISION OF THOMAS NELSON
& ZONDERVAN

Scripture taken from the New King James Version®. Copyright © 1982 by Thomas Nelson. Used by permission. All rights reserved.

Scripture quotations marked (NIV) are taken from the Holy Bible, New International Version®, NIV®. Copyright © 1973, 1978, 1984, 2011 by Biblica, Inc.™ Used by permission of Zondervan. All rights reserved worldwide. www. zondervan.com The "NIV" and "New International Version" are trademarks registered in the United States Patent and Trademark Office by Biblica, Inc.™

Scripture quotations are taken from the Holy Bible, New Living Translation, copyright ©1996, 2004, 2007, 2013, 2015 by Tyndale House Foundation. Used by permission of Tyndale House Publishers, Inc., Carol Stream, Illinois 60188. All rights reserved.

Scripture quotations marked (TLB) are taken from The Living Bible copyright © 1971. Used by permission of Tyndale House Publishers, Inc., Carol Stream, Illinois 60188. All rights reserved.

WestBow Press books may be ordered through booksellers or by contacting:

WestBow Press
A Division of Thomas Nelson & Zondervan
1663 Liberty Drive
Bloomington, IN 47403
www.westbowpress.com
1 (866) 928-1240

Because of the dynamic nature of the Internet, any web addresses or links contained in this book may have changed since publication and may no longer be valid. The views expressed in this work are solely those of the author and do not necessarily reflect the views of the publisher, and the publisher hereby disclaims any responsibility for them.

Any people depicted in stock imagery provided by Thinkstock are models, and such images are being used for illustrative purposes only.
Certain stock imagery © Thinkstock.

ISBN: 978-1-9736-0587-4 (sc)
ISBN: 978-1-9736-0588-1 (hc)
ISBN: 978-1-9736-0586-7 (e)

Library of Congress Control Number: 2017916985

Print information available on the last page.

WestBow Press rev. date: 11/21/2017

Dedicated to my family
My wife, Jennifer
Our children, Joslyn and Jayden

Contents

To My Heroes

To my wife, Jennifer: I could not have been on this journey without you. Next, I must acknowledge my father, Richard; his dedication to me and my family growing up is inspirational and always will be. Also, the rest of my family: we can always learn and laugh with one another.

To my best friend, Sean Conway: he has continually inspired me to grow on a deeper level with Jesus and live fearlessly for the gospel.

To all the pastors, professors, and professionals who have believed in my potential, I want to thank you sincerely for your sacrifices and dedication to your callings. You will always have a hero status to me.
Pastors:

Bill Kingsley, Dan Williams, Charles Semple, Ron Warne, Nick Morasko, Ken Bomberger, Steven G. Carmany, Ken Tinklepaugh (rest in peace), Donald Sadler, Dominic Galati Jr., Andrew Magnuson, Bruce Barnard, Sean Catalano, Brad Whipple, Jay Stillinger, Ryan Austie, and Stephen Mitchell.
Professors:

Dr. Dwight Sheets, Dr. Dick Gruber, Dr. Bruce Marino, Dr. Michael Di Giacomo, Dr. Terry Wardle, and Dr. Don Meyer.
The Professionals:

Thank you to author Jamie Canosa for coaching me and inspiring me to confidently chase this dream and make it a reality! Kelly James of Beauty and Bliss Spa and Drew Kinum photographic artist. Ed Kinnum D.C.

Get Ready!

If you can imagine your life without heroes, you are in grave danger. You are in danger of missing out on your best you. Before you met your heroes, your identity was based completely on only what you could do for you.

Your heroes opened a place in your mind. They revealed something you have that needs to be unlocked: "potential." The heroes in your life helped you unlock your ability to accept your calling. I believe everyone has been given a calling to be a difference maker. That's you!

As you continue to become more like Jesus, you will find yourself ready and have an ordained mandate to no longer live as a civilian but become a hero. God can transform your entire life when you accept His power. Your status will change. You will no longer be a civilian but hold hero status.

Acknowledge Your Heroes

Use this page to write down those who hold hero status in your life. Then take a moment to remember them. Give them a call or even make a special visit and tell them how they were used to help you along the way. As you read this book and remember some of the heroes who were there for you, write their names below. Take a moment to reach out to them, pray for them, and personally thank them.

Chapter 1

BOLD BEGINNINGS

The wicked man flees though no one pursues,
but the righteous are as bold as a lion.
—Proverbs 28:1 (NIV)

"Let's go!"

I couldn't wait one more second. The longer my friends and I stood around talking about going on an adventure, the more restless I became. I didn't want to wait for another day to come and pass. I wanted this day to be our day. I wanted to face our fears and conquer something.

I interrupted again, "Let's go!"

I couldn't wait another second. We lived in a world where checking our e-mails and text messages wasn't part of our daily routine. It was summer; our parents were working, and the only thing that could hold us back was our own second-guessing.

With only our shabby planning, we left for the abandoned limestone tunnel. We'd heard stories about older kids visiting, and we wanted our shot. We wanted to see it for ourselves.

I grew up loving movies where a group of boys got a plan together and set out on an adventure. I found myself living through those movies, dreaming of the day when I would be the ringleader of a group of friends discovering our inner heroes.

While we were traveling to the tunnel on our bikes, I felt him come alive. My inner hero! Excitement bubbled from my gut. I was ready to overcome fear and insecurity by simply giving adventure a try. The seed was planted, and not chasing this present quest wasn't an option.

The Crutch

Excuses are tiresome. For any person who has a desire to take the next big steps in life, learning to resent excuses must become part of your DNA. I strive to be practical; therefore, I understand that in some cases, excuses are completely legit. I will, however, counter that those excuses may have been legit for a season, but you cannot live there. You cannot live by your excuses, or you will never grow. You will remain weak, insecure, and visionless.

You cannot move forward if your boldness doesn't outweigh your excuses. The goal of this book is to inspire you to keep moving forward. Be prepared to start brushing off the dust of any defeat and hold on to determination.

Bolder than Our Blindness

The mysterious tunnel was in the next town over. It was an old, abandoned limestone tunnel used in the forties. It may have only been a few miles away, but it was actually dangerous.

We lived in a section of Syracuse, New York, called Tipperary Hill. To find this tunnel, we had to travel about five miles into a suburb called Solvay. For safety reasons, I'm not going to disclose more information about the location.

The weather was great. It was a clear day. No rain or clouds. It was that nice, beautiful blue sky with a light breeze. We even stopped at a store called Green Front for some snacks. The sun warmed us as we sat outside, enjoying our oatmeal cream pies. The breeze was carrying the enticing smell of fresh pizza being cooked from the pizza shop across the street. Our conversations were fun; we were focused on getting to the tunnel. In order to be bold, we had to focus rather than fear.

It wasn't long after we left from our snack break that we arrived. We parked our bikes and walked over to the entrance, and we simply stood there with amazement. This was what everybody was talking about.

It seemed huge to us. It was about ten feet wide and twenty feet tall. Broken beer bottles and graffiti were everywhere. When you looked into the tunnel, it was as though there were a black curtain draped across it, but we could still see the other side.

The speck of light at the other end was all we needed. We didn't have flashlights. We didn't have any form of safety. We had a speck of light. The darkness created some anxiety within us, but the small speck of light motivated us not to give up.

About ten steps in, we couldn't see our hands in front of our faces. This difficulty challenged us to become bolder than our blindness. Taking cautious steps, we put our hands on the shoulder of the guy in front of us. Our voices echoed off the narrow walls. Although we couldn't see, we kept moving forward.

It's interesting what happened when we started getting closer to the other side. As the darkness faded, our steps became bolder. The light broke the blanket of darkness. We stopped tiptoeing and started running! We ran for the light. We celebrated the light! Our cheers sounded like a team that had just won the championship game. The feeling was one of victory. We didn't let the darkness stop us from celebrating in the light!

CELEBRATION

Struggle leads to celebration. One morning as I walked to my class, I met a guy who seemed "out there." It was too early to be joyful. It was a cold, wet day, and he was humming to himself. He was also singing random words to the song he was humming. Yeah, I was annoyed. My first thought was, *What kind of coffee does he drink?* A few weeks later, I realized I was still annoyed by him. Since I didn't want to hold a grudge, I asked him if we could get lunch. My goal was to value our differences.

As we talked, I learned why he was so joyful. He said, "I don't always feel good. In fact, I have many hard days. I was addicted to drugs and sex for years. I went to a church service, and those addictions seemed to lift from me. It was all the power of God."

I realized he lived as a truly free man. He was free from any earthly bondage. He was dancing and humming and loving his life. He was celebrating.

The addictions had held him in bondage. He had to battle them to overcome. But with this new light in his life, any new struggles were seen as opportunities to discover a new joy. New struggles are an opportunity to unlock new joy.

The apostle Paul faced many situations that, for most of us, might rank in our top ten things we never want to experience. He could unlock new joy even while being literally locked up. The trials Paul faced pinned him to the floor. They brought him to his knees. And he praised and thanked God for them. The struggles quickly shaped into opportunities. He didn't become angry with God, but he sought peace (Philippians 5:5–9). This magnificent example helps us to recognize that we are always in place and set up to embrace a new boldness.

What Is a Hero Status?

A hero status is a report about your bravery. It reveals what you could accomplish under conditions you may have felt were impossible for you. It could be caring about someone who was in need. It could be making room in your schedule to spend quality time with your family. It could be your determination to end an addiction. Either way, your life circumstances are unique to you.

No matter what hardships or letdowns you have faced, you can always look for ways to be bold and change your current situation into a magnificent one. You can be poor, depressed, broken, and even busy. With that being said, you can still make a lasting difference.

Where do you start? In the book of Psalms, David said, "In the day when I cried out, You answered me, And made me bold with strength in my soul" (Psalm 138:3 NKJV). Your hero status starts with the ultimate hero! Let the presence of God lead you to move, crawl, walk, and then run.

I realized I was up against a mountain, and I had a simple yet powerful prayer: "Jesus, I cannot do it without you." Even when I lacked strength and motivation, they were given to me. When I look back on many situations, I am still in awe of what I have been able to overcome. Certainly, as I pray for all of you reading this book, you will be able to look back and be in awe of what God brought you through. And you will also be able to look forward, see the huge opportunities before you, and be bolder than ever!

The Value of the Book of Daniel

The book of Daniel reveals ordinary men dealing with extraordinary circumstances. As I looked at the character of Daniel and other men who were committed to the God of Israel, I saw this theme. They all faced incredibly difficult situations, overcame them, and became heroes.

The book of Daniel also reveals something that is applicable for today. God is in control even when we feel like we don't have a handle on our situations. God can motivate us and strengthen us to overcome our hardships and accept that His plan is unfolding before us. He does this through His continual presence and His sovereignty, ultimate power, and ultimate authority. We can look at every crazy situation we face as no match for God! This ultimately becomes the confidence we need to be bolder than ever. If at this point—the beginning—you think boldly, you will live boldly.

Daniel's Bold Beginnings (Daniel Chapter 1)

Besieged.

For Daniel, this word meant having every ounce of comfort he had ever known taken away. He was plucked from his homeland and forced to serve this very disturbed king, a king who made unrealistic demands of his advisers. Daniel, who was considered to be nobility, also had to stand before him.

A young man having to face certain death if he could not answer the king's question correctly, Daniel took this opportunity to be bold. He boldly sought God for answers. He boldly faced the questions and the tasks. He boldly stood before the court and the guards.

Daniel chose to exchange comfort for boldness. When you read Daniel 1:8–16, you learn of this distinct boldness. If he was going to survive, he needed to be ready to win. He had to completely trust God. He had to reach for God's wisdom and strength.

When you read Daniel 1:19–20, Daniel persevered and came to be recognized as one the most valuable assets to the king. It's exciting to see that even the king celebrated Daniel's boldness. Daniel's boldness completely stands out.

Do you honestly think you are an asset to your workplace? Or marriage? Or children? Are you going above and beyond to provide value to every environment you're part of? You're the only one who can answer that.

Working a job where you feel disposable, dumped on, and even unappreciated is difficult. You lose energy, which means you lose your ability to be bold.

Becoming bolder is a practical goal. It isn't a ticket to becoming unteachable. It is a challenge to become invincible, always being your best!

THREE BOLD ENEMIES

1) Procrastination

If you don't get started, you can't start. "If anyone, then, knows the good they ought to do and doesn't do it, it is sin for them" (James 4:17 NIV). Your ability to make a difference in any environment starts when you start. It's that simple.

2) Price

This can be an enemy of boldness if you don't put enough value on your dreams and ambitions. You set the budget for change. It can be like the antique your grandmother left in the attic, containing great worth, but it's forgotten about and neglected. Or you can dust it off.

If you place value on being bold, then do it. Did you know you're able to humble yourself and be bold at the same time? It seems like a contradiction, but it's not. Humbling yourself before God actually sets you up to be promoted. "Humble yourselves before the Lord, and he will lift you up" (James 4:10 NIV).

3) Priority

When's the last time you made a list of personal priorities? Writing everything down, from what you want to accomplish with your career to your family to your hobbies. What is important? Look at your list, and ask the hard questions. How can I be bolder in each of these areas? As you process your priorities, the giants become smaller, and you will see a transition from stuck in crisis to living like a conqueror.

I am constantly inspired by music. There are hundreds of songs that speak to my heart and my circumstances. Music has a way of speaking to me in a way nothing else can. In a pivotal moment of my life, the song "Learning to Breathe" by Switchfoot made a lasting impression on me. The line from the song that just about knocked me out of my chair, was "I am learning that You and You alone could break my fall" (Jon Forman, Switchfoot, *Learning to Breathe,* 2000). Try again! Fight again! Chase my dreams again! An excitement came over me to dust myself off and live boldly again! Every person can be motivated no matter what the circumstances. Music was used as a tool to send me straight back to the Word of God, and it's the Word of God that truly makes me bolder. I know some people have said they have needed quiet time, do something outdoors, work in their garden, paint, and play music. Often when our priorities are out of sync, the first thing to go is what helps you to relax and think.

Personal priorities should often be evaluated. There are concrete priorities, and others can be flexible. Concrete priorities aren't determined by how you feel emotionally. This is a solid conviction. You won't and cannot compromise. For this to be a constant, you must strive to be constant. The development comes from constantly learning, strengthening, and applying the values to your life. Sadly, we have concrete priorities in our lives and have no clue why.

Flexible priorities may be seasonal. There might be a time where you are going through a transition and must do things you wouldn't normally do. It is easy for people to make defensiveness a priority; maybe during this time, having all your guards up feels good. Asserting yourself is important, especially if this season calls for you to set boundaries. There is a point when you must relax. I love the liner from the movie *What*

About Bob? The doctor's advice is for Bob to "take a vacation from your problems" (Frank Oz, *What About Bob?* 1991). When I heard this, it made me realize there are many people who haven't taken a vacation from their problems, defensiveness, and emotional wounds. This is a practice that is not easy. How do you relax when dealing with a health crisis? A betrayal? Trouble with your children and spouse? Making ends meet? Let's take a vacation from our problems by taking the weight off our shoulders. Let's break a lie; you are not your problems, and your problems are not you!

During these different and difficult seasons of life when you are able to focus on concrete priorities or flexible ones, there is one concrete priority that must remain the most constant. The wisdom of the book of James says, "Submit yourselves, then, to God. Resist the devil, and he will flee from you. Come near to God and he will come near to you" (James 4:7–8 NIV).

THREE BOLD VALUES
1) Relationships
Having a quality relationship with God and people matters. Relationships that encourage you to be your best are fuel. They move us forward. Having an encounter with God's love empowers us. Being cared about and showing others care in return gives us strength to keep going.

One afternoon, I was walking down the street. A man approached me and said he was hungry. I don't let people go hungry. I bought him a couple slices of pizza. As I sat with him, I thought, *This guy is desperate. He needs to encounter a quality relationship.*

I started sharing with him about God's amazing, huge love. He was quiet and then he started crying.

He said, "Thank you for this pizza. I asked you for two slices because I'm going to eat one now and bring the other home to my wife. She has cancer, and she was actually hungry today. She wanted a slice of pizza. You didn't know this, but you were so willing to sit with me and talk about Jesus. I can't pay you back, but I needed you today." We sat in this pizza shop and prayed.

Together, we sat in the pizza shop and prayed.

I'm not sure we always recognize the need for relationships. We're busy and full of mistrust. God created relationships so that we can boldly love others and be a person who is able to create value rather than suck the room dry.

2) *Wisdom*

One of the first places people downsize each other isn't below the belt; it's above the shoulders. If you've ever had to overcome a learning disability, the struggle is real. Discovering how to keep information in your brain is a challenge.

Bold people are discounted when they can't match their boldness with wisdom and knowledge. Boldness is created when wisdom and knowledge take flight. James gives us a practical step to follow if we lack these things.

My favorite go-to verse comes from the book of James. It states, "If any of you lacks wisdom, you should ask God, who gives generously to all without finding fault, and it will be given to you. But when you ask, you must believe and not doubt, because the one who doubts is like a wave of the sea, blown and tossed by the wind. That person should not expect to receive anything from the Lord. Such a person is double-minded and unstable in all they do" (James 1:5–8 NIV).

3) *Timing*

When I played baseball, I hated striking out. I knew for a fact I could hit the ball over the fence. During some of my batting practices, the outfielders would stand on the other side of the fence to return them. During the game, it was a whole different story.

I struggled with timing. It wasn't that the strike zone changed; I didn't grow six inches. The pitcher's windup changed. If you ever go to a baseball game, watch the different pitchers as they deliver. Each is different.

The longer I could watch a new pitcher before I went up to bat, the better my chance to get a good hit. You will not be able to predict every problem that comes your way, but you can work on how you stand up to the situation. You can face it or run away and hide.

Don't wait to learn and be stronger. You're not being a bully for facing your problems! Don't get me wrong. In some cases, the problem you're facing just doesn't need to consume your emotional energy. The truth is, some of our most regretful arguments may have been something minute and petty. Take a moment, and be determined to be your best. It means you could be wrong, or it means you might learn you are opposing your fear and anxiety and becoming stronger. However, if you are called to be the difference maker, be your best and be bold.

Practice your timing. Don't respond to e-mails or messages right away out of anger. Learn to be okay with getting your timing right. Bad timing can lead to unnecessary arguments and drama. All could have been avoided if you committed to timing it better.

HERO STATUS: BEGINNINGS

At the beginning of your life, you were carried. You learned to roll and to sit up. You soon learned how to pull yourself up to a stand. As you learned to walk, you were carried less. You bumped into things and fell over. Each step of your progress happened in small steps.

Your journey is just beginning. You will learn how to move, crawl, walk, and even run! The reason you need to consider this is because if you're at the beginning, need a restart, or are simply bored with your current situation, there is still time. The best time in your life is right now!

Learning how to be bold, especially in the beginning, will seem shaky. You'll at times have to dust yourself off and try again. You will face reminders of your weakness. When that happens, remind your weakness of your bold future. Then be bolder than ever. This is the beginning of your hero status.

Chapter 2

BOLDER THAN BABYLON

Be on guard. Stand firm in the faith. Be courageous. Be strong.
—1 Corinthians 16:13 (NIV)

"Look forward!"

One evening, my wife and I decided to go on a late-night date. It was a nice night. We even drove with the windows down. We could feel the cool night breeze and look out into the streets of downtown Syracuse without the glare of a window. For many years, the downtown area of Syracuse has been improving, and we enjoyed it as a great place to go on dates.

One of my favorite places down there is Clinton Square. During the winter, there's ice-skating and dancing fountains during the summer. Our date started there. We walked around and talked. The tranquility of the fountains gave us time to just relax and enjoy each other's presence.

We could've sat by that fountain all night, but we decided to get something to eat. We didn't go far. We didn't want to stay out too late. So after visiting a nearby shop, we headed back to the car.

As we walked, I had a strange sensation come over me. A little voice told me to look behind us. I could see a man walking toward us, but it didn't cross my mind that we were being followed. After all, this was the city. People walked in the same direction all the time.

Turn after turn, I could no longer ignore his continued presence.

I calmly instructed my wife to continue looking forward and then informed her of my suspicions. Of course, she turned to look, anyway. "Look forward," I reminded her.

My car was parked on a side street. An isolated area. The man behind us was just waiting for us to make that mistake. To get us out of this pickle, we had to find people.

The street we were walking down didn't have any shops. He started walking faster. We started walking faster. We turned onto another street, and I saw a group of people ahead of us, standing around, talking. Safety.

I'm an extrovert, so walking up to strangers and starting a conversation isn't difficult for me. The closer we came to the group, the farther back our would-be attacker fell. As we approached them, the man pursuing us stopped. He turned and went in another direction.

OVERCOME

"Just get over it."

I know I've used this phrase to encourage others I care deeply about, but unless it comes from someone you're close to, it can come across as cold and heartless. Let's be honest; overcoming illness, heartbreak, failures, and addiction is easier said than done. I've met individuals who put their entire emotional life savings into a relationship and ended up bankrupt when things didn't work out. If I'm being transparent, I was one of them.

Overcoming Is an "I" Thing

Only *you* can determine whether you're ready for a serious life change. This means you're no longer comfortable with how you've been traveling through life thus far. But change isn't easy. It takes hard work, dedication, and only comes when you experience success.

I've spoken with many people struggling with addiction. They often reveal to me that nobody believes they can change because their success isn't permanent. They're clean for a couple months, and before you know it, they've relapsed. This can be discouraging; months of success stolen by one bad year, month, week, day, or moment.

"My family doesn't trust me," one young man said.

He went on to tell me that he keeps going to rehab, yet he finds his way back to the drugs and alcohol. He was broken during our conversation, and I found myself growing angry. Not about the drugs and alcohol, but because he didn't have one person in his life who believed in him. Every bridge had been burned—by him. He used up all the grace his family and friends had to offer. He was right; nobody trusted him.

I wondered, *What can I do to help him? He must make this change.*

He told me story after story, and I quickly realized that he was in front of me for a reason. I was going to be the one person in his life who would be a friend and give him what he really needed to hear: the cold, hard truth.

"I believe in your potential." I poured the passion I felt for this young man into my words and went on to speak not of judgment but of focus and hope. Of goals for the future. I refused to back down. Refused to let him look to the past and allow his excuses to have more value than purpose. I made it clear that from this point on, he needed to, "Look forward!"

Three years later, the same young man saw me walking to my car. He was in another vehicle, and he jumped out and ran at me full force. He gave me the biggest hug. I couldn't even move my arms. He didn't give me a chance to hug him back.

He said, "Joe, I can't get your words out of my head, and I'm accomplishing things."

He went on to tell me about how close he was to reaching goals, everything from a high school diploma and a driver's license and even his hope of college. I was completely blown away that I played a role in his life.

Overcoming is an I thing. Until you take a step in the right direction, you will be constantly wrong, standing still. You must be able to admit, *I* was motivated. *I* decided *I* wanted to overcome. *I* surrendered to God.

The first step to overcoming anything is an I thing. You might say, "I am going to get a better job." "I am going to love my family." "I am going to help others." This is certainty the first step.

13

Self-realization makes you take off the mask. Hiding and fear are no longer the bullies. You can no longer say, "I am a fake or a failure." From now on, make it clear, "I live with a future."

REARVIEW MIRROR

Our failures aren't meant to be badges of honor. The lessons you learn from them are. And you can't learn from your failures if you are leaning on them.

Some lessons are learned in an instant. Mom says, "Don't touch that; it's hot." You touch it, you get burned, you learn. But others take time. A delay in learning from your mistakes, even repeating a few of them, doesn't mean you're broken. It means you're *human.*

Your humanity isn't an excuse to keep making mistakes. Your humanity is your excuse to become increasingly dependent on God for strength. You need wisdom concerning your past and to guide you in building your future. Proverbs reveals this refreshing view of wisdom. It states,

> Know also that wisdom is sweet to your soul; if you
> find it, there is a future hope for you and your hope
> will not be cut off. (Proverbs 24:14 NIV)

Sometimes when a person experiences trauma in his or her life, it takes years to recover. Everything from a disappointing relationship to being fired from a job can leave you feeling broken. These hurts can be lasting. Even though the moment has passed, each glimpse in the rearview mirror is still painful.

If you have any thoughts that you aren't good enough, this is going to be your calling to keep brushing yourself off, learning from mistakes, and working toward getting it right. Your painful memories aren't the end of you. They are the beginning of your new beginning.

Proverbs 24:16 (NIV) states,
> A righteous man falls seven times, he rises again,
> But a wicked are brought down by calamity.

What about looking back and remembering our beautiful memories? I have had conversations where people have tried to be humble about some of the highlights in their lives. They almost take an unhealthy humility and never talk about the good times. There are people who only remember those great memories and never learn from the hard times.

So what is it? How do we stay joyful? How do we live in a humble way? How do we use our experiences to be bold?

The rearview mirror of your life is like looking at a small glimpse of what you just passed. There isn't anything wrong with it. You can see what is behind you. But the windshield in front of you is a lot bigger. Your best view is through the windshield. The glimpse of the past helps you stay focused on the future.

Like driving, you aren't driving safely if your eyes are focused on the rear view. The past is a mix of joy, laughter, heartache, and sorrow for us all. Revisiting it can bring us knowledge, happiness, even peace for a time, but don't get stuck there. Don't spend so much time looking in the rearview mirror that you forget to look forward!

DANIEL (DANIEL 2)

Daniel is a key example of looking forward. He was trapped in Babylon, taken from his home, and placed before one of the most irrational kings on earth. The king demanded that sorcerers, astrologers, and besieged wise men interpret a dream he had. They were to prove themselves by interpreting the dream without being told a single thing about it.

Impossible.

Daniel 2:1 reveals the king was troubled in his mind and could not sleep. The king's logic was irrational. It could have been due to his sleep issues, but his demands were indeed impossible.

Daniel was chosen by God to overcome the evils of humankind. He was the only one in the kingdom able to unlock the mystery. Daniel boldly sought God for the answer. He prayed and praised God and was given the answer. Then he presented it to the king. Daniel said, "No wise man, enchanter, magician or diviner can explain to the king he asked about but there is a God in heaven who reveals mysteries" (Daniel 2:27–28 NIV).

When Daniel shared his truth with the king, I am sure everybody, including the king, was speechless. Daniel's captivity in Babylon did not stop him from boldly seeking God's answer.

Logically, nothing in Daniel's life to this point makes any sense. This was a serious, life-changing event. He was besieged, stolen, and kidnapped. He lost everything, including his family. He lost his comfort and security. He was stripped down to himself and whatever he had inside him.

It was what was inside him that saved him. It was Daniel's extreme trust in God and the favor that was bestowed on his life. The image of Babylon is a dark one, but there is no situation too dark for God to change.

After Daniel reveals the dream, the king falls "prostrate"; he placed himself facedown. The most powerful king in the land had just met his match. Daniel was a hero. King Nebuchadnezzar responded to Daniel by saying, "Surely your God is the God of gods and the Lord of kings and a revealer of mysteries, for you were able to reveal this mystery" (Daniel 2:47 NIV).

The king did not only acknowledge Daniel's God as the God above all. He revealed his trust in Daniel so much that Daniel was given power within the land. God can take a slave and make him a prince.

God can take you, an ordinary person, reveal your divine purpose, and make you a hero.

DNA

Your DNA defines you. Scientists can take a single strand of your hair from a crime scene and perfectly pinpoint you as the suspect. It is who you are. But what if your DNA was left at the scene of greatness?

Now is your chance to leave your mark. It's time to prove what you're capable of and to stop letting obstacles stand in your way. Stop looking in the rearview mirror. Stop leaning on the past. It's time to push forward, and discover a new great season. The future is what you choose to make it, but only *you* make that choice. And keep making it. Every day.

What does DNA stand for? In the world of science, DNA means deoxyribonucleic acid. Yeah, that's a pretty cool scientific word. It says a lot about what you are. It's more than whether your future kids might be blonde, brunette, male, female. This is your genetic identification code.

What if your everyday actions created a sequence that could be traced back to you? Actually, your actions can be. From where and when you update social media to where you drive and spend money. So if people can be put on trial and convicted based on their DNA, can you be put on trial and convince the jury that you are living every day bolder than ever? Do you have a hero status?

D—Drive
N—Nobility
A—Alignment

Your hero status DNA can tell you even more about yourself. It touches *who* you are, your unique abilities, character, and personality. Your capacity to overcome and look forward.

Let's take a closer look at DNA.

Drive

I was diagnosed with the autoimmune disease Lupus. The hardest part about this disease isn't the pain; it's the effect it has on my drive. I'm a task-oriented person. I like to work hard and get things done. When this disease is roaring, it attacks that drive. It tempts me to give up. Motivation can be hard to find. This diagnosis is a constant reminder that I can't afford not to know what drives me.

Your drive says a lot about who you are and what you're capable of. If you dig deep and strive to accomplish something, *anything*, then you will. But if you aim at nothing, you're simply throwing things on the ground.

It's sad to see so many people with no aim. God made each of us unique. Each of us has a purpose, something to accomplish with our time here on earth. Don't throw it on the ground. You're not here by mistake.

Focus. Aim. Accomplish.

Your drive level is something that you need to examine and reexamine constantly. Know where you're going and what motivates you to get there. Keep looking forward.

Nobility

One evening while in a checkout line, the man ahead of me became upset about the store's policy regarding his purchase. He was using vulgar language and letting his temper get the better of him. I couldn't believe the way he was speaking to the person working at the register.

There was nothing noble about that man in that moment. He thought himself justified in creating a scene. But rather than gain what he was after, he lost the respect of those around him.

Nobility isn't signing up to be a doormat. Nobility is signing up your character to make righteous decisions. Choosing to create peace in moments of chaos. To be constant when everything around you is inconsistent.

In our most emotionally charged moments, we must stop and ask ourselves if we are being noble. When I look back on this moment, will I like what I see? This is the only way that growth can take place.

Alignment

In college, one of my roommates let me borrow his car. It didn't take long for me to notice that it was in desperate need of an alignment. It was a little unnerving knowing that if I let go, I'd soon be hitting a guardrail.

I often meet Christians who tell me they want to live a life perfectly aligned with the Word of God. That's great! I wish we all had that mindset. Yet, there's tension that often comes with this.

The tension is created when your objective to follow God's word is performance based and not relationally aligned. This is where the greatest commandment challenges us to align ourselves with the word of God.

Learning to make building and maintaining relationships a functional part of your everyday life is huge!

Your Babylon

Life may have been fairly easy for you thus far, or maybe you've had to sweat and bleed for everything you have. Either way, your past is a part of who you are. We all have a Babylon that we need to be bolder than.

It's your story, and today is a blank page. God is wise and loving enough to encounter you wherever you are. Place your trust and focus on Him moving forward.

What part of your story would you like God to be more of a presence in?

Hero Status: Perseverance

Our perseverance reveals the hope we have inside. If people are impressed, great! If people ask you about your hope, even greater! If you are able to help someone take big steps to have the hope you have within, the best!

Your life is not a mistake, no matter how many regrets and failures you think you have. You may feel like you're broken and can never be fixed, but you are wrong!

Let the wrestling match of life begin. Let your life carry this amazing hope that others need to see in you. If your goal is to blend in, you won't be seen. But if your goal is to be a world changer, then you're going to look for ways, big and small, to be a hero for someone else.

May God teach you to unlock your hero status!

Chapter 3

BOLDER THAN THE BLAZE

Now, Lord, consider their threats and enable your servants to
speak your word with great boldness. Stretch out your hand to
heal and perform miraculous signs and wonders through the
name of your holy servant Jesus. After they prayed, the place
where they were meeting was shaken. And they were all filled
with the Holy Spirit and spoke the word of God boldly.
—Acts 4:29–31 (NIV)

"Push!"

I was still in shock that I'd made the varsity football team as a tenth-grader. Every day I worked hard to prepare for the upcoming season, excited to do whatever the coaches asked of me. I knew I had a long way to go to become the best player I could be.

One day after practice, the coaches handed out discount cards for the team to sell. They told us to go out into the community in groups and raise money for the program. The guys I got grouped with were all older. They were all friends already. And I was the new guy.

We stuffed into Steve's car and headed north because he worked on that side of town. When the gas light turned on, we all volunteered to chip in to help fuel our journey. But when we pulled into the station, we quickly realized something wasn't right.

We were parked beside a gas pump, and the engine was smoking. But we must have been in shock because no one realized what a potentially dangerous combination that was. As we stood around, trying to decide what to do, a couple of police officers happened to stop at the gas station for coffee. They saw the smoke and jumped into action. Shouting out instructions, they yelled, "Push!"

The possibility of an explosion forced those men into action. They were motivated to help because danger was imminent. The blaze was motivational.

YOUR TURN

"Impossible!"

"Why me?"

"It's not fair!"

I've heard these words from teenagers, parents, and even my own mouth. There are thousands of car accidents every day. Also, millions of burglaries every year! Hate crimes, school shootings, and terrorism are on the rise. The world can be a scary place. And yet, when faced with a traumatic experience, people are always stunned that it could happen to them.

Trauma is subjective. We all experience and deal with it in different ways. As an adolescent, we begin to learn what trauma means. We learn coping mechanisms, healthy and unhealthy, as we seek a path to regaining control. Teens turn to everything from self-harm to isolation and acting impulsively.

As adults, our coping mechanisms can be even more drastic and lonely. Relationships, jobs, marriages … they're all impacted by past abuses, health issues, stress, and so much more. We long for relief! We long for peace! Why wouldn't we?

Sometimes we all just need a pause button. A vacation. A break. A moment to get away from it all and just breathe.

This is your moment. If the past few years have been wearing you out, if you don't know who you are anymore, if you've lost all sense of purpose, this is for you. Push!

Or maybe this isn't you. Maybe life has yet to throw you a hardball. You may think that you don't know how to console someone going through something you could never even imagine. That it's the scars that connect us. But that's not true. It's life that connects us. This life that we're all living. Together.

Perhaps you're meant to be the patient friend, the listening ear, the shoulder to cry on that they need. And one day in the future, when this life pitches you a curve, you'll be prepared to push.

POWERFUL YOU

There is so much power inside you. A force that you bring into every situation. An ability to connect and influence in ways that are uniquely yours. Some people have told me, "I don't understand why I tend to feel alone in a group?" "I am not sure I fit in." Or rather than say a single word, they just quit.

Just you being part of the group brings life to it. Without you, the room would be completely different. There is no one like you. There can never be a duplicate, and you can never be replaced. You can be dumped, divorced, and fired, but that doesn't change you. That doesn't change your potential.

When I was in college, I lost a pet. I was devastated. Many friends offered what I'm sure they thought was excellent advice. It started out kind but grew annoying after a while. They may have experienced a similar trauma, but not *my* trauma. They weren't *me*. They didn't lose *my* pet. And they didn't cope the same ways I did. The scars were similar, but no two are identical.

One of the most meaningful things someone did for me was finding me on a bench in the middle of campus, sitting beside me, and saying, "I've never lost a pet. I don't have anything to say that can help you feel better. Is it okay if I just sit with you?"

My friend provided this presence, but after he left, I continued to sit there. That was when I felt the healing begin. "Surely God is my help; the Lord is the one who sustains me" (Psalm 54:4 NIV). Some of the best encounters with God are the ones where I feel like I can just be still. Where I don't feel an urge to check the time or look at my phone.

The power of my friend's presence helped me feel supported. This need was met. My spiritual need was met a few moments after he left me. I needed to breathe. I just needed to be able to take a deep breath and feel one moment when I didn't want to grieve but just be still.

Sometime afterward, I felt like I was catapulted into helping others get on their journeys to healing.

THE SECRET TO YOUR PRESENCE

Just be.

You don't need world-class wisdom. No dictionary of sage words necessary. You just need to be. That's all. Be there. Be silent. It's okay to say, "I have no idea what you're feeling or thinking, I can't imagine. Do you mind if I just sit with you?" And listen.

Not everyone will say yes. Everyone copes in their own ways. But there is power in the offer.

WHEN DO YOU PUSH?

Life moves forward. Always. Whether we want it to or not. Whether we're ready to or not. And there comes a point when you can no longer stall. You can no longer hide. When grief, despair, pain, and fear need to be overcome. A point when you need to push!

You need to wake up and take care of that crying baby. You have to find a computer and start applying for new jobs. You have to attend the funeral of a friend or family member. It isn't easy, but it's time. It's time to push.

I believe you can do it!

There was a night when I considered quitting the ministry. I wanted to walk away from everything. I'd just experience an incredibly painful incident at a church I was working at, and I lacked the strength to keep pushing.

It was about midnight. I was watching television because I couldn't sleep, trying to numb myself to the situation, when a man I knew sent me a message, asking me to call him. It was the middle of the night, but life had already turned upside down, so I dialed his number.

When he answered, he told me, "I don't know why I have to tell you this now, but I felt like you needed to hear it."

I wasn't really sure what he could possibly have to tell me that could make any difference. I'd already made up my mind.

To quit!

To give up!

To stop pushing!

Tears clogged his voice as he explained, "Three years ago, God used you to change my life. I didn't believe in Jesus as my Savior, but now I do. Because of you. Whatever you decide to do, don't quit."

Those words: "Don't quit."

I sat there in silence for a few minutes, until he asked if I was still there. There were tears rolling down my cheeks. I told him that I was and that he was right; I'd needed to hear exactly that, exactly then. That's when I realized I was experiencing a push moment.

Push moments don't make things easier. They don't shrink the size of the mountain you have to climb. They simply provide fuel for the journey. They mean you're ready for the healing to begin.

THE FOURTH MAN (DANIEL 3)

What makes this story even more amazing than three men surviving a fiery furnace was the change of heart of King Nebuchadnezzar. There were three Jews who had been with Daniel since the beginning, and they would not compromise their commitments to God, even if it meant death.

The king made a huge statue; it was made of gold and ninety feet high. The orders were for all persons to bow and worship this stature when they heard the music play. The king loved this because his ego and pride were completely out of control.

There were three men who did not bow and worship this statue. They were Shadrach, Meshach, and Abednego. They were spotted by some of the king's astrologers and turned in for not participating.

They were faced with submission to the king and his idol or death. They stood their ground. They proclaimed to the king boldly they didn't care, and they would not worship the idol.

They said,

King Nebuchadnezzar, we do not need to defend ourselves before you in this matter. If we are thrown into the blazing furnace, the God we serve is able to deliver us from it, and he will deliver us from Your Majesty's hand. But even if he does not, we want you to know, Your Majesty, that we will not serve your gods or worship the image of gold you have set up. (Daniel 3:16–18 NIV)

Denied! They didn't care either way. They would never submit to a false god. They were truly committed to their God, and nothing could and would change that. This was their boldest moment before the king. This is when they crossed the line from being good to stepping into the realm of great! From this point forward, their boldness made them legends.

The king did not take this well at all. He ordered them into the furnace. He believed they would be consumed by the heat and die at his command. The king was mistaken. They did not die! They were not consumed by the fire. To the face of the king, they told him their God would deliver them, and He did!

The king's utter disbelief that these men would be saved from the fire brought him to a place of amazement and wonder. For him to look down at the furnace, he must have known his own soldiers died carrying out his orders. When he looked down, he didn't just see Shadrach, Meshach, and Abednego; he saw a fourth man. They were unharmed, and the flames did not touch them.

The king's response was,

Praise be to the God of Shadrach, Meshach and Abednego, who has sent his angel and rescued his servants! They trusted in him and defied the king's command and were willing to give up their lives rather than serve or worship any god except their own God. (Daniel 3:28 NIV)

He took his enthusiasm to the next level with the next verse. He was astonished at what just happened. He realized their God was more powerful than he was. Instead of protecting his pride, possibly even

25

kicking these men out of the kingdom, he was enthralled by their God's power and accepted it. He makes a decree that leads you to believe not only was he amazed by this power but wanted everyone to lavish in the power of their God. He states,

> Therefore I decree that the people of any nation or language who say anything against the God of Shadrach, Meshach and Abednego be cut into pieces and their houses be turned into piles of rubble, for no other god can save in this way." Then the king promoted Shadrach, Meshach and Abednego in the province of Babylon. (Daniel 3:29–30 NIV)

MEASURE

Can you measure boldness? Is there a scale? Can we even compare one person's boldness to another's? I don't think we can. We can only measure boldness on our own scale within our unique being.

We can measure our reactions. We can say we reacted poorly or even boldly. I can even support someone saying, "I reacted bolder than I ever have before." Many times, if we look for a measure, we can measure with "push moments."

We say things like, "I worked really hard." Other times, we could say, "I was passive." Intense people, although motivated, even need a scale to measure. They may find themselves having to be bold all the time, but there is still an amount of push pressure that they need to reflect on.

No matter what type of personality you have, you are going to face push moments. Let's be prepared for them.

PUSH MOMENT PREPARATION

The first way to prepare for a push moment is to prepare yourself to *need* a push moment. This sounds silly, but it isn't. You need to be aware that strange, stressful, and sad moments are parts of life. There's no magic spell that can keep us from experiencing pain and disappointment at some point in our lives. No magic words that can get us through the hard times. What gets us through is loyalty. And faith.

We can't run from God when we're hurting. We can't hide from God when we're struggling. We can't escape Him at all because He is always there. What we can do is commit that if we must go through a season of turmoil that we will take each step with God. We will allow Him to show us the way and provide us with the fuel—push moments—we need to make it.

The second way to prepare is by helping others. Take the time to listen to others who are hurting. Take the time to learn how to be a presence. And take the time to learn to pray. For yourself as well as others.

It is often encouraging to hear that someone is praying for us. Sometimes showing up on a doorstep with prayers and hugs can be a comfort. Other times, a person may need his or her space. That's okay because prayers can be said anywhere by anyone at any time. Maybe now isn't the right time for your presence. Be patient. Wait. And keep praying. Pray out loud. Write your prayers in a journal. Lift them up. You can do it!

The third way to prepare is by building friendships, small groups, or your own life team. There are people we absolutely need in our lives—family, close friends, the people who know us better than we know ourselves. The ones who are completely honest and encourage us to be our best.

If your friendships are more like a revolving door, it's possible that you're choosing poorly or not open enough to allow your relationship to be a two-way street. It can be scary to open up to others and letting them see who you really are, warts and all. But you need to give as much as you get, or you'll have no foundation on which to build.

Upgraded You

Ask yourself,

Are you a better version of yourself than you were last year?

How about a better version than when you were in high school? College?

On your job?

With your family?

With your faith? With God?

Whenever my computer needs to upgrade, it forces me to step away and do other things. Sometimes I talk with a coworker. Other times, I clean my office, restructure my schedule for the week, or read a book. The system needs to be upgraded because it's running slowly, but this puts me in the position to make strategic choices.

"Upgrade, I need to upgrade." Say it out loud. You need to. You need to remember what works for you, and keep growing and developing.

Time is our most precious commodity. It's the one thing that once spent, we can never get back. Spend it wisely in ways that will help you upgrade. Look for mentors, build relationships, and overcome challenges.

And don't forget to include the fourth man. Bring God into your time. Include Jesus in your circumstances. Let Him provide the push you need in every hardship that you face. Let Him be part of your past, present, and future.

HERO STATUS: PUSH

Your personality says a lot about how much push you are willing to give in any situation. If there is an accident, will you be the first to dial 911 or assume help is on the way? If your marriage is struggling, are you going to wait for the other person to change or break up? Are you afraid to confront your child on his or her reckless behavior, or will you avoid the confrontation because having another argument is tiring you out?

Your push moments will come, and they weren't meant for you to live in discouragement or wear you out. They are meant to motivate you. There is no fire hot enough that God cannot protect you from.

Transform your life to hero status. You can do it! Surviving the blaze is the beauty of boldness.

Chapter 4

BOLDLY BENT

Trust in the Lord with all of your heart and lean not on
your own understanding; in all your ways acknowledge
him and he will make your paths straight.
—Proverbs 3:5–6 (NIV)

"I can hear the road."

Every summer my family camped in Wellesley Island State Park,
located on the St. Lawrence River on the boarder of New York and
Canada. This was a great place for us to vacation. It gave us a few days to
get away from the city and spend time swimming, fishing, and hiking.
My uncle even had a boat we used to travel up and down the river,
checking out the different islands.

One afternoon, my father took my brother and I on a nature hike.
We'd been hiking for about an hour when we decided to take a detour
from the trail to climb a hill. Somehow, we got really turned around.

After some time, I asked my father, "Are we lost?"

"No," he answered. "We're just looking for the road."

Which, of course, meant we were lost. But I wasn't worried. My
father was an ambitious man. I knew he'd get us back to camp somehow.

From up on that hilltop, the thick canopy of leaves blocked the road
from view, so he told us to listen. "Close your eyes, and listen for cars."
If we could find those, we could find our way home.

My brother and I stood very still, and we listened. Nothing.

"Let's go in this direction," my father said. "Maybe we can hear better down the hill."

So we walked some more, following our father through a thick, almost marshy terrain. Both of us grumbled and complained. We were hot and tired of walking. The ground sucked at our shoes, making the path he'd chosen difficult to follow. But our only option was to trust our father. Separating would only make things worse.

As we pushed through some tall grasses, our father stopped us and told us to be quiet. He listened. "I can hear the road!"

We weren't lost anymore. There was a way. A path. A direction to follow.

As we continued along behind him, the sound of tires whizzing over concrete grew louder. Exhaustion took a backseat to hope, and we caught our second wind. A few miles along the side of that road brought us right back to our campsite, and I couldn't wait to tell our story.

ARE YOU LISTENING?

Throughout the Bible, there are many places that describe God's voice. It's been called thunder, raging waters, earth shaking, and even a whisper. The Bible also reveals that God's Word is powerful enough to shape the universe and separate soul from body. But the only way to hear it is to listen.

Are you listening? Are you paying enough attention to the things that will lead you in the right direction?

When you feel lost, it's easy to panic. To try and find your own way. When the path gets hard, it's easy to want to veer off in another direction.

My father was older and wiser than we were. He knew what it would take to get us out of those woods and onto the road. Finding your way through life takes exactly the same thing: the ability to listen.

The hard part is knowing *who* to listen to.

WHO ARE YOUR REFERENCES?

When you're looking for a job, you need good references. You want someone who's able to sell you to a company so that you have a better chance to be hired. Choosing the right people to speak about your future is important.

Not all your references have your best interests in mind. They are given a confidential moment to honestly speak on your behalf. Picking your references is a big deal. In the world of Job searching, it is absolutely critical to know your references and have a solid relationship with them.

It still puzzles me how some of us can trust three or four people with the fate of our careers, yet we can't trust others enough to speak to our personal development. Trust is a difficult thing. I have learned if I am going to learn to trust, I need to also understand how to overcome betrayal. Betrayal glues itself to your soul. The memories can be lasting, and moving on can feel impossible.

Your references won't let you lie in the muddy waters of life. They want you to have nothing less than a hero status. They will dust you off when you fall, and cheer you on when you succeed. Let the *right* voices steer your path.

Where are the few good people who can speak to your heart?

Choose wisely.

THE BENDING BRANCH

I was a Boy Scout for many years. I've always loved the outdoors and having friends to explore it with. We often visited state parks and nature reserves. On one such trip, we went for a hike led by a park ranger. As we made our way through the shadowy forest, he pointed something out to us that I've never forgotten. A ray of light.

A single ray of light was coming through the leaves, reaching all the way to the forest floor. Nearby was a young tree—only a couple years old—and it was bent. It was bending toward that ray of light. The tree naturally wanted to touch this fresh sunlight. It wanted to grow no matter what was surrounding it.

There are times in life when we have to bend. We have to become bent on the truth, against bullies, and on doing the right thing. That is boldness. It's exciting!

Picking the Right People

Every relationship you form is a risk. There are people who might love you one minute and leave you the next. You cannot control what other people do. That is a fact. There are a few steps that I encourage others to take when they're pursuing any kind of relationship.

The first step: listen to what they say about others. Which way are they bending the truth? Is it true? Can trust be developed? If they're speaking poorly of others on a regular basis, believe me, you are on their list too. It's like a boomerang.

The second step: drive on a two-way street. The value of any relationship is give and take. Good friendships blossom from mutual investment. Expecting others to do all the work is selfish. Let's call it the way it is; good friends want to give just as much as they receive. It is a joy to bless you and be blessed by you.

The third step: stop thinking instantly. Are you looking for lots of shallow relationships or lasting ones? If you're looking for lasting relationships, you must be committed to the process. There is beauty in the process. You learn what they like and don't like. You learn about their families, and they learn about yours. You share joy, and you share grief. The process will reveal whether or not the relationship is a "you haul" or a "long haul." Is it a frying pan or slow cooker? Lasting relationships take time and patience, and these relationships can be more fulfilling than short-lived ones.

Overcoming the Wrong People

Trauma

Trauma is more common than we like to believe. One afternoon I was at a playground with my daughter when I noticed a bunch of scuffmarks at the bottom of a slide. They were made by children who had learned that if they didn't try to stop themselves, they wouldn't stop until it was too late.

Many of us have emotional scuffmarks. We have trust issues because of a bad relationship. Or we fear making friends in a new work environment because we were fired from the last. Or we're constantly defensive because of being bullied.

I have spoken with people who have different fears that have turned into phobias. I have met people whose families were robbed when they were children, and now they have locks and alarms on everything. My grandfather, who lived through the Depression, would always go out and buy milk and butter whenever there was a chance of a snowstorm.

So often we carry baggage into our workspace, relationships, and even friendships. We have dealt with a type of trauma, and rather than wrestle with it and learn to overcome it, we let it control us.

Every relationship you enter is a risk. You risk being hurt and let down. Everyone who enters a relationship with you accepts that same risk. They are risking being hurt and let down by you. It's more mutual than you think. So the risk of having a relationship turn traumatic is a real thing. How many times have we asked ourselves, "Why?" "Why am I still emotionally invested in a relationship that left me empty-handed?" It's because you cared, trusted, and saw potential and had no return. You cannot just accept it; you need to heal and learn. And the more you heal and learn, the more you will discover that the care and trust you show others is authentic and creates value.

My goal for this section is to help you take a confident step toward being bold. To do so, we cannot ignore the importance of inner healing. I believe your restlessness is no match for the Holy Spirit. There have been times when I was prayed over, and the first thing God did was deal with my restlessness. From that point on, I could face life's challenges with a clear mind.

Healing from trauma can take time. I am not opposed to counseling. I think many Christians undervalue the importance of this. There is no question that God heals and restores instantly. For many of us, our journeys toward being whole again requires us to be coached and counseled.

COUNSELING

By not dealing with your trauma, you are burying your inner hero. I met a lot of people who are using their past hurts as a driving force. More often than not, I also see these people burn out.

My first suggestion may be upsetting to some: counseling. It's amazing how many people look at it as taboo when the entire focus is to guide you toward being clear minded and healed. Many dedicated counselors tell me that people make so many excuses why they don't need counseling. My encouragement is this: please don't use humility as an excuse to be lazy. Be determined to uncover your inner hero. If your past hurts cause you to miss out on living your life boldly every day, you need to deal with them.

EMOTIONAL WEIGHT

When you give something emotional weight, it has control on you. The first time I went hiking with a heavy backpack I felt the pressure on my feet. It slowed me down.

The same occurs when we are carrying something around emotionally. It keeps us from being bolder.

One afternoon, I saw a group of people going from house to house in my neighborhood. For a very long time, I have gone into every encounter with the intent of being able to pray for my guests before they leave my home.

I quickly learned our theological differences were much deeper. This was the first time that I was ready to kick someone out of my house on the spot. There was an emotional trigger that these people pressed in me.

I asked if I could pray for them, and the woman snapped, "No, because I don't know whom you are praying to. You don't know God." In other words, it felt like she was saying, "You are inferior to me."

What do I do? How dare she tell me I can't pray in my own home! I was angry and soon realized I lost my concentration. I could feel myself become warm. I couldn't let my defensiveness or the emotional weight that I felt stop me. Within a few moments, I was able to mentally regain my composure, keep my character, and respond.

For this encounter, it was not a two-sided relationship. It was her word against mine. I quickly responded, "You're going to tell me that I have to sit here, listen to you, and take your literature, but I can't pray for you? This makes no sense."

She repeated herself, and that was when I showed them the door. Not because her beliefs were different than mine, but because the relationship was one-way. She made it very clear that nothing I stated was of value to her.

Relationships and influences need to be two-sided, so you can recognize the value in each other. We want to like our friends for their admirable acts and their quirky humor, and vice versa. Sustainable relationships recognize the maturing of the relationship comes with time, communication, and mutual encouragement.

What do we do when we are in a one-way relationship? This is a big question because I want to respond based on Matthew 18, where instruction is given to work toward restoring a relationship after an offense. Each situation is different. Friendships, marriages, families, and workplaces are unique to every person and every situation.

We often look for the answer that affirms our struggle is real and makes us feel most right. This can be drastically wrong if you try to fix your marriage this way. You're not fixing your marriage; it's more like trading problems. You can only move forward if you ask the right questions of yourself. "Am I really praying about this?" "Am I expressing my gratitude?" "Are my expectations unreasonable?" "Am I improving?" "Am I learning?"

It is important for you to be in healthy relationships. If your struggle is becoming dangerous, seek a counselor in your area or a specialist who can give you long-term care and guidance.

THE DOOR

The door is a commonly used symbol. For many, it is seen in a negative way as in being kicked out, unwelcome. But you have to pause and consider if being removed from one situation is simply a shove in the direction you were meant to go all along.

Stop. Listen.

It may be hard to swallow, but maybe this is a bold moment given to you in an uncomfortable way. You might feel sore, angry, and discouraged. There is time for a trade. Trade self-pity, and strategically rethink it. You are in the realm of opportunity!

I've met many people who were adopted. They had a door closed on them when they were just babies. Their birth parents wouldn't or couldn't care for them for whatever reason. In many cases, I've seen these children grow up in amazing homes, go to college, and have great careers. They may not have chosen to have been given up by their birth parents but in retrospect, it was the right path for them to follow.

How great is our God that no matter our situation, we have the opportunity to discover our inner hero? That He takes the time in each individual's life to show us the way. If only we choose to listen.

There are times when we must make the choice to close a door. Whether it's an abusive relationship or a toxic environment, this can cause us grief. We can feel like failures. Afraid of change. Afraid of the future. But then there's hope. People who come to understand the rightness of their decisions are able to go on and help others shut doors. Heroes!

Opened Eyes

I can't imagine a life without heroes. A life without people ready to fight for what's right. I cannot imagine a life where people have stopped trying for the impossible. I cannot imagine a life where people stop believing in a bold today and an even bolder tomorrow.

I can imagine weak people becoming strong. I can imagine slaves being set free. I can imagine the fake being real. I can imagine the complacent becoming bolder than ever. If it's your dream, do it! I am telling you to chase it!

Acknowledged (Daniel 4)

In Daniel chapter 4, King Nebuchadnezzar's eyes were opened. Daniel interpreted his dream, and everything Daniel told him came true. The once-mighty king faced humiliation. He was described as a homeless man with long nails and nasty, messy hair. The door was shut in his face; his kingdom lost. And he was humbled.

This wasn't the end of his journey, just a shift in direction. A new path. A new possibility! His trials bent him toward the light. He recognized God's kingship and exalted and gave glory to God in heaven.

This was a bending moment, where the truth was leaned into and brought into existence. It is powerful and exciting.

BENDING, NOT BREAKING

Have you ever heard the words, "You might be bent, but you're not broken"? Have you been able to live in the moment, understand the hurt that is before you, and still hang on to God?

This is about survival. You cannot do this alone, and you shouldn't let others around you go through it alone, either. Learn the practical needs of others and yourself. Be a person of action. Be a hero!

HERO STATUS: SURVIVAL

Your survival matters. Your future matters.

Take some time, and get to know who's on your team. Know what making a difference looks like. Know how to face past trauma and overcome it. But most important, do whatever it takes to listen for the road.

Listen for God to direct you and then have the faith to follow. Be bent for boldness! Make your hero status known!

Chapter 5

BREAKING BAD BOLDLY

As soon as I pray, you answer me; you
encourage me by giving me strength.
—Psalm 138:3 (NLT)

"This is our neighborhood."

The new babysitter's house was prime real estate. Up the block was a corner store with a variety of candy for only a few cents, and I had a pocketful of change. I couldn't wait!

Some friends also went to the same house to wait for their parents to get out of work, but on that day, I was the first to arrive. I didn't waste any time. As soon as I hopped off the bus, I asked if I could go to the store, and she agreed.

As I walked, I noticed a group of boys who had just gotten off their bus across the street. I noticed them because they were all huddled together, talking and casting glances my way. I picked up my pace, but before I could gain any distance, the boys started running at me, shouting, "This is our neighborhood," and, "Get him!"

I soon found myself surrounded. I spun around, looking for an escape, but there was none. There was nowhere to go. No one to help me. So I decided to try and talk my way out. I tried explaining to them what I was doing there, thinking that might help. No such luck. One of the boys pushed me from behind. The others started shouting, calling me names. Another sucker punched me.

Then I heard, "Y'all better back off!"

A much older man seemed to have appeared out of nowhere. A wooden baseball bat hung from his fingers, and he pointed it at the boys. "If you try to jump another kid in my neighborhood, I'm going to jump you."

The boys sized up the old man and his wooden baseball bat. Slowly, they began to back away from me.

The old man waited until they'd crossed the street and gone their separate ways before telling me, "Nobody's going to get jumped by them in my neighborhood again."

SURROUNDED

It's difficult to remain calm when you're surrounded by chaos. There are days when problems can make you feel like the walls are closing in on you from all sides. Like you're struggling just to get your head above water, only to break the surface and find yourself surrounded by sheer cliffs.

Surrounded! You're surrounded. One step away from giving up the fight and letting yourself sink back below the waves. I've known many people who have sought different types of relief in these seasons of their lives. Some as drastic as suicide.

Breaking the bad in your life takes boldness. And help. Every relationship in your life affects you, even if you don't realize it. They either encourage you to push for greatness, or they don't.

One afternoon, I was talking with someone I considered a friend when I had an awakening. Something the person said struck a chord, and I realized that the trust I'd put into the relationship wasn't being returned. I went back to the person and asked, "Am I only a joke to you?"

I confronted the individual's attitude and took the opportunity to defend myself. I don't like to be confrontational, but in this instance, I had no choice. I would no longer suffer in silence. For the longest time,

I'd ignored similar remarks. I'd laugh them off, while inside, they ate at me.

Until I mustered enough courage, the issue would never be dealt with. It took boldness to confront the real issue. It reminded me that there are two sides to this. We take back control and deal with the issue, despite the outcome. Or we stop giving in to silence and say something.

RESCUE

When you find yourself in serious trouble—the life-threatening kind—you don't question the person there to save you. You wouldn't say to a firefighter, "No thanks. Don't save me from this burning building." Or to a lifeguard, "Thanks, but just let me drown." You accept the help offered, and you're grateful for it.

When I think back on that day when I was surrounded, I often remember the boys' aggression. But more so, I remember that old man's boldness. I didn't tell him to go away and mind his own business. I didn't ask him to exchange the bat for a flyswatter. If he could have rolled up in a tank, that would have been great. He offered to help me, and I accepted. And I was glad he was there.

So then, when it comes to sin, why are we confused about salvation? Why are we arguing with God in the burning building? If sin is an anchor, pulling you below the waves, why fight grace bringing us to the surface?

When grace meets sin, it saves. When grace meets weakness, it saves. When grace meets past failures and future fears ... still, it saves. Sin is a powerful, destructive force, but it is no match for grace.

Grace runs into burning buildings. It dives into rocky waters. It stands up to bullies with a baseball bat. Grace doesn't play fair. It isn't politically correct. It isn't neat and tidy or logical. Grace doesn't back down! Grace is bold! Grace is the reason you can be bold today.

When your sin shouts, "Guilty," grace whispers, "Free." You can pile every sin you've ever committed into one giant heap, and with one word from God, it's erased: "Forgiven."

FORGIVEN

Why are so many of us afraid to be bold because we have a portfolio of past mistakes? Why do we second-guess ourselves? Why do we wait for someone else to jump in? God didn't forgive you so that your past could stand in your way. God forgave you so that you can shine.

Jesus didn't do all that He did and sacrifice all that He did so that we could walk in weakness. He did everything so we could be a shining example of His greatness.

Forgiveness is about being humbled, not haunted. When I think about John's word, he declares, "God is Light: in Him there is no darkness at all" (1 John 1:5 NIV). The darkness wants to haunt you. The darkness wants to steal the full-fledged confidence that only forgiveness gives.

I can always tell when I've met a person who's been forgiven a lot. It can be scary and fascinating at the same time. The sin in the individual's life held him or her down like a dog on a leash. It made the person a slave. Stole the individual's identity. But forgiveness set the person free. It allowed him or her to cut the leash and run. The person has this amazing inner energy and a true sense of who he or she was meant to be.

THE WRITING ON THE WALL (DANIEL 5)

Chapter 5 introduces a new king. His name is King Belshazzar, the son of King Nebuchadnezzar. It appears that Belshazzar ignored his father's mistakes and ruled at his own leisure.
In the middle of one his parties, something spooky happened. Imagine being surrounded by people, celebrating and drinking wine, and all of a sudden, words begin to appear on the walls. The movie *The Shining* always comes to mind when I read this.

Daniel was brought to the wall and asked to interpret it, but it was already too late. The words were a warning of the king's death.

They read,

> God has numbered the days of your reign and brought
> it to an end. You have been weighed on the scales and

found wanting. Your kingdom is divided and given to
the Medes and Persians. (Daniel 5:26–28 NIV)

So what do you do with that? How do you take in the reality of this situation? There was absolutely no hope in the writing on the wall. It was a death sentence. The king ignored God, and it cost him everything.

YOUR WRITING ON THE WALL

I wish looking for the answers to our big questions was easier. We're all different. We all need our hearts and minds to sync. If they don't, an emotional, off-center state of mind can create a mess.

There's a reason people are warned not to make big decisions when faced with a crisis. After a loved one passes, being fired, or even a bad breakup, we want to shed that sadness as quickly as possible. We want to feel free. So we're more prone to make risky decisions. Decisions that can have lasting consequences.

I'm not telling you that you should look for the writing on the wall. I'm not telling you that you should let others interpret what the writing means. I'm telling you to write on your own wall!

Now, before you go out and buy spray paint and Sharpies, let me explain. What I mean is that you should look for opportunities to do things that are greater than you've ever experienced. When going through a hard time, we need to look for chances to express gratitude and be generous.

You might feel angry, lied to, sabotaged, shamed. Trust me, I understand those feelings. But don't let them stand in your way.

Not long ago, I had two major life-changing events in one week. I was let go from my job right before the holidays, and I had to find a new place to live. It all happened so quickly I thought I was going to lose my mind. For days, I was a zombie. I couldn't focus. Couldn't have a rational conversation. I was stuck. Paralyzed.

To break free, I had to dig deep. Using words like "please" and "thank you" didn't come easily. It was hard to show people that I appreciated them when I felt so unappreciated. But I started to look for ways to be generous with my time, which I suddenly had a lot more of.

A friend needed help with a room he was finishing, so I went to his house and completed as much as I could before he got home from work. He was so grateful. And it was in moments like that, moments when I found ways to be generous, that the writing on the wall—which read, "I'm a nobody," "worthless," "failure"—began to fade. Those dark feelings still needed to be fought off periodically throughout my job hunt, but I was no longer setting myself up to fail. I was setting myself up to feel restored and renewed. Ready to move forward.

Rebel against the ridicule! Believe it or not, there are lessons to be learned from your troubles. Don't forget them. Let them teach you to be a better, bolder person.

EDUCATED

Foreign languages are not my strong suit. It takes me hours and hours to memorize new words. I failed Spanish twice. I doubted it would ever be possible for me to do well in any language class.

That doubt was blown away by a professor I had while working on my master's degree. He taught Greek in a way that made sense to me. No memorizing vocabulary and boring drills. He explained that it was highly unlikely that I'd ever use Greek as an everyday language.

He went on to say, "I could require you to memorize vocab and allow this to use up your time, or I could teach you how to research and find the answer even if you're miles away from the seminary."

This made sense to me. He taught us how to be ongoing-learners. I may not always know the words, but I always know how to find the answer.

Life is a series of questions. Not all of them have answers. I don't know why your child passed away. Or why you were abused. I don't know why you have a debilitating disease. Or why you lost your job. I don't know why your relationship ended. But I do know what you need. Closure. It's what we all seek in lieu of unattainable answers.

Closure doesn't come through anger, resentment, or guilt. Those emotions are weights. They drag you down and keep you from your bold destiny. Closure comes from forgiveness. It comes through healing and time.

Don't give your enemies the upper hand. Don't let the mockers smile. Make them fear you and all that you are capable of. Take the weights off. Throw them away. Bury them in the sand. Learn to recognize the capable you. The you that strikes fear in your enemies with your potential. Take a moment to remember who you are.

At times, you may feel down, but you aren't. Your enemies will fear you.

HERO STATUS: PERSPECTIVE

God didn't spin the world and say, "Good luck." Remember the very powerful words Jesus spoke:

> You will receive power when the Holy Spirit comes on you;
> and you will be my witnesses in Jerusalem, and in all Judea
> and Samaria, and to the ends of the earth. (Acts 1:8 NIV)

Our perspectives have to change. Why are you settling for second best? Your life is meant to be lived with power. You are meant to be bold!

The writing on the wall can say two things: "Success" or "Struggle." It can say, "Be little," or, "Be bold." In either case, don't give up! The strength you gain from overcoming your weaknesses will be something you and others are going to be inspired by.

Struggle points to success, and your success can be credited to your struggle. You win! Nothing can hold you back. No fear or failure can interfere with your journey to be bolder.

Remaining content isn't a hero status; it's an excuse. Rewrite the writing on the wall. If Jesus has given you hope, then the world has one more hopeful person pointing hopeless people to the greatest life they can live and the most amazing reward when they take their last breaths. You were born to have a hero status. You were made to be bolder than ever.

Chapter 6

BOLDNESS BEFORE BEASTS

You will tread on the lion and the cobra; you will trample the
great lion and the serpent. "Because he loves me," says the Lord,
"I will rescue him; I will protect him, for he acknowledges
my name. He will call on me, and I will answer him; I will
be with him in trouble, I will deliver him and honor him.
—Psalm 91:13–15 (NIV)

"I raised my arms and yelled!"

One of my friends had been away all summer. He got to be part of
a Boy Scout wilderness camp experience, and he shared with me some
of their adventures. We talked about how he helped some of the boys
at camp overcome personal issues and even coached them to getting
their merit badges.

I had been in Boy Scouts for a while and had many great memories
of my experiences. I'd also gone on a wilderness adventure, but I thought
the stories he shared with me were hilarious.

I sat and listened to his experiences as he waved his hands and even
reenacted things. One story in particular sounded like a mix of bravery
and insanity. He said, "On one hike, we could see a black bear down
the path. My hiking buddies were scared. But I wasn't. I raised my arms
and yelled. I yelled like a madman!"

I'm not sure what the people in the pizza shop thought when he raised his arms and ran back in forth in front of our table. I laughed so hard. If I were a bear, I would have run away from him too!

As I thought about his story, I realized that I didn't have that kind of boldness. In my years of Boy Scouts, we learned to fear these animals. We were taught about the danger they posed. Fear was planted in our minds and grew until it held us back, keeping us from hiking down bigger and more exciting trails.

KEEP AWAY

There's a point when you have to finally come to terms with the fact that you need to keep away from certain people, environments, and even positions. It's not that you can't be a witness and a light in the darkness, but the darkness is sneaky.

It puts you in a box and steals your momentum. You see, there are two ways to deal with bears. You can raise your arms and yell or curl in a ball to protect yourself.

There are some situations you won't be able to escape or relax in. I've often found that people who have lived in a box of fear are offended over everything I say or do. I recognize that this is a problem.

I'm an extrovert, so if you're an introvert, I promise I'd scare you. I admit this in a humble way. If you're a serious introvert, my extroverted personality would likely cause you to become uneasy.

All of us were raised in different homes. We come from different towns. We have different struggles. We also have different "beasts." We face life from our own angles. This is perfectly okay. We are all original, and there's a fantastic chance you're better at dealing with different problems.

There are boundaries to setting boundaries. Sadly, I have seen some people with such tight walls that others are quickly cut out. Friends and even their own families are shown the door the moment a situation becomes uncomfortable.

I'm going to take a moment to be controversial. I don't believe there are people who deserve to be close to you. I'm not giving you permission to be arrogant. I'm simply encouraging you to maintain your momentum.

I've met many people with problems. Many had issues that eliminated the possibility of trust between us. It didn't mean they were outcastes. It meant there had to be a civil agreement between us. We would be polite in public, but it didn't mean we had to have a conversation or ask about each other's families.

To some of you, this may sound harsh. Biblically, we are given an approach on how to deal with conflict, and sometimes, the Bible is extremely harsh. So what do you do? In some cases, we go to the offending party privately. In others, they're kicked out of the community. Since I am not writing a manual on how to interpret Matthew 18, I'm going to give you some practical ways to maintain your boldness and composure.

WHO TO AVOID

Manipulators

First, recognize them. This is the hardest step. Whether they realize it or not, they're selling you a broken product. They're telling you what you want to hear. It often takes time for manipulators to be unmasked.

Second, set boundaries. The relationship you once had is broken. You could have been lied to or betrayed. This isn't easy to overcome because it often leads to heartbreak and disappointment. You spent a lot of time building trust, and suddenly, you find yourself back at square one, trying to figure out what was real and what wasn't. Someone once told me when he realized a friend was manipulating him, it took years to get over it. At times, he felt like he was going out of his mind. It was after this he started being diligent about boundaries.

Third, hold onto truth. These are the moments you're forced to think about truth. I often read Philippians 4:8–9. This passage is incredible to meditate on, especially if you've been in a situation where you feel like you've been manipulated. Manipulators and thieves rob you of the peace of God and your self-worth.

The passage states,

Finally, brothers and sisters, whatever is true, whatever is noble, whatever is right, whatever is pure, whatever is lovely, whatever is admirable—if anything is excellent or praiseworthy—think about such things. Whatever you have learned or received or heard from me, or seen in me—put it into practice. And the God of peace will be with you. (Philippians 4:8–9 NIV)

Take a moment and read this passage. It gives you a chance to personalize whatever is taking up unnecessary space in your life. If you're thinking, *Easier said than done,* you're right. This does take work, but I promise you the work will pay off. When you're able to live with a mind of redemption, you get to a place of boldness, which God has been preparing you for since birth. Has anybody told you lately you're not a mistake? Has anyone spoken words of life into your ears that penetrated your mind? If not, it's time to listen.

Green-Eyed Monsters

Jealousy exists for everyone from elementary-school children to professional businesspeople. "Keeping up with the Joneses" is nothing but a competitive face to jealousy.

Jealousy can be lethal to any relationship. People who struggle with jealousy are tempted to make their lives, houses, positions, children, and social statuses look better than yours, regardless of your feelings. Your discomfort brings them pleasure.

Those sassy smiles, rolling eyes, cheap-shot comments, and silly grins are signs they're looking at you through their scope, ready to shoot. It's scary stuff. On more than one occasion, I've felt the sting of betrayal. Many times it was rooted in jealously.

So how do you set up boundaries between you and the green-eyed monsters? This goes right back to the second of the greatest commandments: "Love your neighbor as yourself" (Luke 6:31 NIV). It's not wrong for you to call out someone for aggressively or passive-aggressively acting jealous toward you. You might feel awkward or like you are entering a childish conversation. The reality is you really could be entering a childish conversation, and it might be on the other person's end.

Unless you can find the root of the tension, it's likely to continue to exist. Jealousy not confronted is destructive. When it is confronted, it can be redemptive. You may have someone in your life who needs you to affirm you care about him or her and the person's stuff and struggles. The person needs to know you want to discover ways to be happy for each other. When the individual does well you feel happy for him or her, and you want that in return. Can you imagine if everybody learned this in elementary school?

In some cases, you can't fix the problem. This is when the only healthy step available is to end the relationship because one side refuses to budge. Relationships are two ways; they are not meant to be one-sided battles. When it is, you must find an opportunity to make the boundaries clear.

Arrogance

The quickest way to lose sight of your mission is by allowing arrogant people to be your advisers. You're welcoming them to put a blindfold on you. They will tell you, "You don't need to see the poor because they're all drug addicts. You don't need to help a struggling family because they just keep making mistakes." Arrogance teaches you how to ignore.

While at a conference, I overheard a fellow attendee speaking about someone from his congregation. She had physical issues, which created a problem for her to get to and from church, so she reached out to her small-group leader. Rather than encouraging the relationship and teaching patience and compassion, he described her needs as an extreme case of manipulation. I couldn't believe what I heard. It was appalling to me that he was encouraging and teaching people how to be arrogant!

To this day I wish I spoke up. I have a daughter with a disability, and if a church doesn't honor her presence in its congregation, you won't see me there again.

Compassion is a big deal. You cannot be bolder in your workplace, school, or relationships if you ride the wave of arrogance. Your boldness is not going to be taken in a positive light. In fact, you might start being the one who is avoided by others.

So how do we avoid catching arrogance? What can we do if we know we're arrogant or borderline? There's a fine line between being a leader and a boss. When you understand your position, you can tweak it to get the job done and motivate your employees without being arrogant. But if you are going to grow past the temptation to be arrogant, you must investigate your heart. It's time to start asking the tough questions.

"Do people believe that I care about them?"

"Do I believe that I care about others?"

"What stops me from caring authentically for others?"

Lion's Den (Daniel 6)

Ever since I was a kid, I've loved the story about Daniel and the lion's den. I grew up about two miles from the Burnet Park Zoo. This zoo is fantastic. They had lots of different animals. Recently, they got an octopus. But my favorite part was always the lions.

The lion enclosure was pretty big. It didn't matter where they were hanging out, you could see them. They'd often be sleeping, but what made them so majestic was when they paced back and forth near the crowd.

As a child, I thought if there wasn't this protective glass between them and us, we would be so dead. As an adult, I took my children to the same zoo. Of course, I was excited to see my favorite exhibit: the lions!

While watching these lions pace back and forth in front of us, I had the same thought. I might be a lot bigger now, but the prey these powerful animals hunt and eat in the wild are even bigger than I am.

When we think about the story of Daniel and the lion's den, we might recall the children's books where he's in the pit, and the lions are nice and yellow and cute. I don't think that was the case. Lions aren't pets. They were wild beasts kept by the king, so he could witness people being eaten alive.

The officials targeting Daniel in this story were jealous because his anointing caused him to gain favor with God. That part of the story is familiar to anyone who has had to deal with toxic people. It could be anyone in any social circle. Even people we love dearly can create friction. They make it impossible for you to live freely, targeting you because they fear you won't line up according to their rules. You don't fit their mold.

Daniel kept his faith firm even under pressure. He still prayed. He refused to back down. Amazingly, King Darius prayed for Daniel even in his judgment, saying, "May your God, whom you serve continually rescue you" (Daniel 6:16 NIV). And it was Daniel's faithfulness revealed that saved him!

How can you fend off lions? I'm not sure there's a manual for that like the one the Boy Scouts used to teach us about bears. But as Daniel reminded the king who sentenced him to death, God is stronger than any earthy beast or bully.

YOUR LION'S DEN

Your "lion's den" is something you need to be mentally prepared for ahead of time. If you feel pressure from your job or with family members, it's good to have a game plan. It's good to know who you'll be in those situations. If you're going to be anything, be yourself. Be you! Be a strong, bold you!

STRONG, BOLD YOU
Define Your Layers

Understanding your layers is kind of like understanding how to make lasagna. I'm not sure if there's a right or wrong way to build lasagna, but there are different elements that serve different purposes.

Sauce, noodles, and cheese are the main ingredients, but everybody has their own style and may even add different ingredients to make their recipe unique.

You are unique. You have layers. You have some essential elements to your layers, like body, spirit, and personality. But you have other layers, as well. Other "ingredients" unique to you. Rather than ignore them and try to be like anybody else, define your layers. Understand why you're serious all the time or why you love to be lighthearted. Understand your relationship with God, and accept the fact that you experience seasons where God feels close and others when He seems distant. Understand your body; are you healthy or dealing with sickness?

Your unique makeup is what makes you, you!

The Tough Guy

My daughter has Down syndrome. When she was about a year old, I saw her do something unexpected. She had these chubby cheeks and a toothless smile. She had the superpower to melt your heart when she was happy. And if she was upset, she would make a sad face that made you feel like your heart literally just broke inside your chest.

One day she was at the grocery store with me. When we got in line to check out, a tough guy got in line behind us. He fit the description of a biker. He had a sleeveless leather jacket, long goatee, and lots of biker tattoos. He didn't make me nervous, but he was difficult to miss.

I had to step in front of the cart to put the groceries up to check out. Joslyn was an arm's length away, so I didn't mind if this massive guy stood nearby. I kept talking to her as I took our food out.

At first, he just stood there, looking forward. But my daughter's cuteness was determined to break through his tough manner. She stared at him and grinned. He started to crack these little half-smiles back at her. I broke his shyness and told him her name. As soon as I said that, he began talking to her. "Hello, Joslyn. Are you shopping with Daddy?"

Baby talk! He was speaking baby talk! He was smiling from ear to ear, talking to her in a sweet voice. I couldn't help but smile. Then he yelled for his friends to come over. A couple other guys, who looked similar to him, started doing the same thing. I was outnumbered, but I knew what was happening. This group of bikers just wanted to be sweet.

There's something about seeing a big, strong, tough guy become compassionate that completely touches your heart. Some things move you, and it's when you're moved by compassion that you start to see action.

We see children starving in other countries, families breaking up, couples divorcing, homelessness, drug use, and so on. There are so many unique situations that maybe you understand, and it moves you to action. You know how to help. You know what to say and what not to say. This is what makes you, you.

And then there are occasions when our passion seems to jump out at us from thin air. We see something or hear about something that moves us. Sometimes it's as easy as asking someone we've never talked to how he or she is. It's amazing what happens when we have these divine moments that shape us and change us from the inside out.

Without realizing it, my daughter unlocked those men's compassion that day. A lot of times our compassion is unlocked in the same way. It's right in front of us, we need to stop thinking about it and start acting upon it.

If you know what your layers are supposed to look and feel like, this is an opportunity for you to clean them up and start to focus on your passion, renew your schedule, and look for ways to be bolder than ever!

Use Your Layers

Each of your layers serves a purpose. Life doesn't have one plot line. I know some people with incredible schedules, and I can almost set my clock by them. Even these people have to face unexpected situations sometimes and are forced to respond.

Some mornings you wake up motivated, and others less so. In either case, there's still a chance to focus and figure out your goal for the day. Maybe you're overwhelmed and can only manage one day at a time. So be awesome at managing it!

Try this. Write down all your goals. Then, as you go about your day, pray for boldness and strength to accomplish them. When you complete them, cross them out. And make sure you remind yourself that you're bolder now than you were when you woke up this morning.

You can do this for goals, projects, people, and even fears. Take a moment to trust God to give you the strength to silence the bullies and beautify your boldness.

CHALLENGE: PERSEVERANCE

Challenges don't reveal your frailness; they reveal your fearlessness. You can overcome. You can face the day. You can face your boss. You can face your family. You can face your health issues. You can overcome your weaknesses.

The pressure may make you feel like you're going crazy at times, but you can persevere. There's someone out there who needs to hear your story. They need to know you were able to persevere in the worst circumstances. Keep sharing your story. The more you share it, the more you'll want more such moments. Share your bolder-than-ever stories!

Chapter 7

BEDSIDE BOLDNESS

The Lord is my shepherd, I lack nothing. He makes me lie down
in green pastures, he leads me beside quiet waters, he refreshes my
soul. He guides me along the right paths for his name's sake.
—Psalm 23:1–3 (NIV)

"Why are you so stressed out?"

One of my college classes required me to be involved with extra activities. This gave me the chance to visit the inner city of Philadelphia and distribute food and clothing to the homeless population living there. I was a little nervous, seeing as this was my first time going into Philadelphia—aside from taking the bus—and the only time the activity took place was late at night.

The streets were dark, but it wasn't hard to find people. In fact, I was hit with a bit of culture shock at seeing so many homeless people sleeping in the hallways of the subway station and alongside buildings. Homelessness is a problem all over the country, even in my hometown of Syracuse, New York, but I'd never seen anything like this before. I asked myself, "How can this even be possible?"

As we walked around, handing out food and clothing, many people spoke to us. They told us their stories, and we listened. Some of the men and women there had jobs at one point, just like the rest of us. But due to circumstances, they'd found themselves in a catch-22. They couldn't keep a job without a vehicle, but without a job, they couldn't afford one.

They all seemed happy to see us. Perhaps our presence was a glimpse of hope. It may have been some time since anyone had looked at them with dignity. Or perhaps it was the gospel.

I went into that night with a broken heart because a relationship I had high hopes for wasn't working out. When we got to the city, I set all thoughts of that aside and got to work. I remember the sound of the wind rattling a chain-link fence. About halfway down the block was a blue tarp where a man was living.

He was sleeping when we approached but quickly rose when the leader of our group called him by name. It was a skill the others had told us you develop on the street, rising quickly, because they never knew what they'd be facing when they did. The hazy yellow light from the streetlamp reflected in his eyes as he spoke with us. We'd come to feed him, and he returned that kindness with wisdom.

The words he spoke that night have been lost in my memory, but I remember clearly the moment he singled me out. He looked right at me and asked, "Why are you so stressed out?"

It was almost as though he'd read my soul. He saw the brokenness inside me, so I let it out. I told him everything about how my relationship had ended, but my heart still wasn't ready to let go.

He said, "God can fix them, you know."

"Relationships?" I asked.

"No," he said. "Hearts."

My vision blurred. I tried to blink away the tears, but it was no use. I wiped them away as quickly as they fell, feeling like a fool. The man came closer and took my hand. He brought me close, put his hand on the back of my neck, and began praying for me. He asked God to lift the stress that was weighing me down. This man, who had nothing, was praying for *me.* And I felt what I can only describe as peace enter my heart and mind.

THE PEACE OF GOD

People search to the ends of the earth to find peace. They seek it through religion, relationships, material possessions, jobs, friendships, even medication. The pursuit of peace can be a very unpeaceful pursuit.

For many, peace equals control. Not having to fear because every decision that affects your life is made solely by you. That definition of peace is inaccurate and unobtainable. The military exists to keep the peace, but in reality, if there was peace, there would be no need for the military. We need to learn to separate peace and control.

What about peace with God? What does that mean? What does it look like? I've met many people from various religious belief systems, and they often tell me this is what they're searching for. They want to have peace with God, so they practice their religion exactly how they think they should. They go to church because they think they should. They judge others—separate themselves from people who think differently than them—because they think they should.

I think it's all messed up. Many of our belief systems are guided by our insecurities rather than our securities. True security only comes from God. When I read Psalms, I love that when David says, "You are my refuge." He doesn't mean, "Only if I don't have a broken heart," or, "Only if I never get sick." David is making an unconditional statement because he has faced the troubles of the world and understands that God is more powerful than any of them. Amid any situation, God is his refuge.

In the gospel of John, Jesus says, "My sheep listen to my voice; I know them, and they follow me" (John 10:27). Have you ever lived on a sheep farm? Well, I have. The first place my wife and I lived when I got out of seminary was a sheep farm. The fence was about ten feet from our back door. We saw them, smelled them, even found them in our backyard, eating the lawn. But the sheep didn't know us. They didn't trust us. They didn't recognize our voices. So when we walked outside and yelled, "Hey, sheep," they took off running.

One day I heard the shepherdess calling to her sheep. They lifted their heads to listen. When she called, "Sixty-four," sheep number sixty-four came running. Not from her but *to* her. There was no fear. The sheep recognized her voice. It knew that voice meant food, acceptance, and protection. It gratefully accepted all she had to offer because if a sheep was sick or hungry and did not seek out its shepherd, it would eventually die.

When God speaks into our lives and we ignore it, when we allow our issues to come first, are we the sheep who do not seek our Shepherd? When we seek peace on our own, can we ever find it? If we run from His voice, will we ever feel accepted and nourished?

Sheep are prey animals. They do not have fangs or claws or shells to fight or protect themselves. The sheep's only strength is in knowing its shepherd. It is the shepherd who provides the security the sheep needs to be bold. Boldness needs to be backed by confidence.

Feeling confident enough to be bold requires you to get to know your Shepherd. There are many ways to do this because God knows we're not all the same. Some people practice meditation and sign up for yoga classes. I can't bend like that. Others get up early and read their Bible first thing in the morning. Or they spend hours listening to worship music. Explore your options. Keep asking yourself, "What brings me peace?"

What works for others may not always work for you. That's okay. God is one size fits all. He's versatile, and He wants to know each of us the way we are, the way He created us to be: individuals.

God is the greatest force in the universe. He created it to fit our needs. The earth is perfectly aligned with the sun. Other planets serve perfectly as force fields against countless asteroids. And there's a perfect combination of gases and layers to our atmosphere that keep us from suffocating, burning, and freezing. Chemically, biologically, geologically, and astronomically speaking, we live on the most perfectly engineered planet in the entire universe.

With that said, how can we not discover peace? When I was searching for my connection to God, I started taking walks at night to see the stars. I'd take a few moments just to listen to the sound of the wind in the trees. I even started taking pictures of the beauty of nature. That was my time to remember and reflect on the wisdom of God. It was during those walks that I built my trust in Him and His words.

Peace Within

I like watching shows about history, especially documentaries. One night I was watching a documentary about WWII. My grandfather fought in the war, so it's always fascinated me to see what he went through. He spent a lot of time on battleships in the Pacific, cooking or clearing beaches of the fallen bodies of his fellow Americans and enemy soldiers.

He used to love sharing stories about the trouble he got into, his many girlfriends, and some of his more fearful moments. He shared pictures too. Thousands of them. There was a whole table in his house full of pictures that he would write about. My mother even bought him a tape recorder, so he could record his stories with his voice. Being able to look back brought him peace.

Often when he picked me up from school, he'd be listening to oldies. I'm not talking about the sixties and seventies. I'm talking about guys like Frank Sinatra and Dean Martin. He'd sing along, whistling through his teeth as though the songs had just come out on the radio.

I loved spending time with my grandfather. He'd crack jokes and tell me the same stories again and again. One afternoon while sitting at his picture table, we got to talking. He and my uncle had gotten into an argument about religion. My grandfather was raised Catholic, but my uncle found his way to the Protestant church. Both were stubborn in their beliefs, but my grandfather knew just what to say to push my uncle's buttons. After overhearing their argument, I asked my grandfather why he made such a big deal out of it.

He said, "Getting your uncle mad is just something I do. He wants everybody to be one of those 'born agains.'"

I don't know why, but it made me laugh to know my grandfather did this on purpose. So I said, "I'm pretty sure you and Uncle believe the same thing, just call it different names."

He looked up at me over his glasses and said, "What? Impossible."

I made a list and split the paper in half. As I asked questions, he realized just how much they had in common. They were arguing over terminology.

Not long after that, his health declined. My wife and I almost cut our honeymoon short to come back and see him in the hospital, but he recovered. When we went to visit him, we found him chatting away with his roommate. I asked him if he needed anything, and he requested a candy bar. The kind with coconut and almonds. He wasn't supposed to have them, but he was dying, so I went to get the man his candy bar!

As I was leaving to buy the chocolate, he said, "One more thing. I need a comb. There are some dames that keep coming around." He was referring to the nurses. I got him his candy, his comb, and even a bag of chips.

Between my visit and his passing, my father had a chance to speak with him. While they were visiting, my grandfather told him, "I know I give your brother a hard time, but I am a born again."

My father called to tell me, and I realized perhaps I'd played some part in that, and he made sure someone knew. When my father called again the day after Good Friday to tell me that my grandfather had passed away, I felt grief-stricken, but there was also a small sense of peace. I knew that God had called him home exactly at the right time.

For many of us, it's difficult to understand the loss of a loved one. We shed tears through our smiles. Grieve when no one is looking. Nothing seems to ease or fix our brokenness. All we want is peace, but all we feel is pain. We ask ourselves, "How can I be bold or joyful? How can I possibly love again? How will I ever be the same?"

Let me share with you the only answer I have: I don't know. I don't know when your pain and brokenness with lift. I don't know when your tears will dry. I don't know when your heart will begin to mend. What I *do* know is that your boldness hasn't disappeared. It's still there. Perhaps it's resting, taking a deep breath, preparing to face whatever comes next, but it is not gone. You are not done! You will learn to breathe again. You will learn to be bold again.

BOLDNESS VERSUS THE BEASTS (DANIEL 7)

Have you ever had a dream that's distressed you? Often when I'm dealing with things spiritually, my dreams have meaning to them.

Usually I keep them to myself and often feel foolish sharing them with others.

Daniel, who had a reputation of being favored by God, had some abnormal dreams, as well. In one instance, he dreamed of animals and iron teeth. The beasts were being devoured. Amid all the destruction, he said,

> There before me was one like a son of man, coming with the clouds of heaven. He approached the Ancient of Days and was led into his presence. He was given authority, glory and sovereign power; all peoples, nations and men of every language worshipped him. His dominion is an everlasting dominion that will not pass away, and his kingdom is one that will never be destroyed. (Daniel 7:13–14 NIV)

What Daniel saw was a clear image of the coming Messiah. It's one of the greatest images recorded in the Old Testament. This passage reveals God's great wisdom of the fate of other nations and reign of His kingdom.

When Daniel woke, he struggled with peace. He's described as being physically pale. Seeing what he saw created a tremendous amount of anxiety in him. So how does that kind of stress affect us? How did it affect Daniel? How did he learn to be bolder than ever even when he was afraid? We'll see in chapter 8.

GET IT BACK

There will be many times when you'll feel afraid, nervous, or discouraged along your journey. There will be times when you'll face depression. People will surprise and disappoint you along the way. You will feel pride in your accomplishments and defeat in your failures.

What does this mean? It means I want you to be honest. There's no magical formula or theology from the name-it-and-claim-it movement. There is only practical advice on how to be bolder than ever, even when you doubt you can make a difference.

Rest is important. You're not the Energizer Bunny. You need to sleep. Your body and mind need time to recharge. If they don't get it, they crash. If you feel burned out, step away and rest. Exercise, go for a walk, read a book; there are many healthy ways to rest beyond sleeping. Discovering a healthy new you allows you to be bolder than ever.

Even when you can't feel it, your boldness isn't gone. It's just overworked. Give it a break. Sit back. Heal. And then turn that engine back on again, and make it happen!

CHALLENGE: OVERCOME

Now is the time to overcome the challenges before you. Fight back against the darkness. Take back your heart.

One night when I was struggling with one of the greatest bouts of depression I'd ever experienced, I was sitting with a friend who was in the Gulf War. He shared a story with me about a time he'd received a warning from a nearby camp that an attack was on the way. His fellow soldiers were all sleeping, so he ran from building to building, along every floor, screaming and banging on doors, warning them to get their chemical warfare suits on.

As he spoke, I realized that the man beside me was a hero. He saved lives that day. By the time he'd made it to every door, he was so exhausted that he could barely get his own suit on. Tears dampened his eyes as he recounted the details. Standing there with an imminent attack on the way—weary, worn, needing rest—he remembered a promise he'd made to his wife to come home safe. For a long time, when he remembered that moment it was not with pride but regret. He'd broken his promise to be safe when he put those other soldiers' lives before his own.

For years, he didn't feel like a hero, but he revealed to me that over time, his heart changed. He came to realize this moment was his God-given opportunity to be a hero.

I was amazed by his story. Amazed that I had the honor of knowing this man. Of calling him a friend. Even more amazing, this hero chose to be *my* friend. The fact that he could feel regret for something so heroic was eye-opening to me. I decided right then and there that I'd no longer bury myself in self-loathing. Rather, I'd find a way to make a difference. I wanted to look back and feel pride. I wanted to help rescue as many people as I could!

I believe God puts people in our lives to inspire us. You are going to be put in other people's lives to inspire them. Thinking deeply about this cycle amazes me. I often try to make a phone call to or visit people who have inspired me.

Some of us have loved ones who have passed away, and their memory inspires us to accomplish things we never thought possible. We think about them and hold their memory very dear. On the other hand, for many of us, that memory is fading. It's been a while, but we would never be the person we are today without them in our lives.

For anyone who has lost a hero in his or her life, this is for you. Take some time to reflect. Remember your hero and allow that person's memory to make you smile again, love again, and be bold again! Take time to remember. Write your hero's name on the line below, write "Thank You," and sign your name.

In Loving Memory of

_____

Chapter 8

IN THE BUSINESS OF BOLDNESS

*Great is my boldness of speech towards you; great is
my boasting on your behalf. I am filled with comfort.
I am exceedingly joyful in all our tribulation.*
—2 Corinthians 7:4 (NKJV)

"Get off my train."

I was headed west, part of a team on a mission to help teach churches
how to evangelize. I really didn't know what to expect. To be honest, I
was nervous. My stomach was in knots. All I wanted was for that train
to come, but if you've ever had to catch a train in Syracuse, New York,
you know they're never on time. What was supposed to be an arrival
time of seven o'clock in the evening had already been delayed several
hours.

As I waited, I sat on the platform and watched groups of people
arrive and depart. The benches weren't exactly comfortable, intentionally
made that way to dissuade the large homeless population from sleeping
on them. To distract myself from the discomfort, I allowed my mind
to wander. A lot of my thoughts were centered on stress back home and
the desire to get away and find my element. I felt a strong pull toward
adventure and meeting new people. When I look back on that summer,
that's exactly what I experienced.

Finally, my train pulled into the station, but by this time, tensions were running high. The woman in front of me began arguing with the man collecting tickets. He looked tired and angry. There were raised voices and name calling. When she tried to push past him to get on board, he yelled, "No you don't! Get off my train."

His eyes flashed to those standing impatiently in line behind her, and he explained, "I have been awake for almost twenty-four hours, and anyone who wants to start trouble on my train isn't boarding."

As security escorted the irate woman away, I think we all learned an important lesson. We really just wanted to get on the train and mind our own business. I handed him my ticket, found a seat, and tried to sleep.

WHAT ARE YOU IN THE BUSINESS OF?

No matter where you work, it can be a stressful environment. A man told me his boss yells at and criticizes him on a daily basis. He says he's learned to live with it, but at first, he stayed up late, thinking about all the things that were said to him. He wanted to shut it off, but he was giving it too much emotional space.

Some have called this the "breaking process." They are slowly being worn down by unkindness as they struggle to support themselves and their families. They shut down emotional responses and simply learning to work on autopilot.

Others are unable to detach work from home. I have worked several odd jobs where I lived in constant fear that each day would be my last. Indecisive management would put me on pins and needles that carried into my everyday life. It's an extremely difficult position to find yourself in.

How do you leave a job that is providing for your family but robbing you of your emotional health? This is very common.

Often, we invest a large portion of ourselves in what we do. In fact, back in the day, many people made their professions by their last name. Do you know someone with the last name "Shoemaker" or "Baker"? Odds are one of their ancestors worked that exact job.

My mother-in-law was a police officer for her entire career, and we like to joke that she may have retired from her job, but she will always be a detective. On many occasions, people will greet me as "Pastor Joe." For them, it doesn't matter if I am working in a church or not. They believe I have the heart of a pastor. and I can't help but be compassionate. What are *you* in the business of? What you do to make money will naturally say something about your behavior. For a majority of your week, this is your role. Look at your day. How do you prepare the night before? How do you drive to work? What do you do to unwind on your way home?

How can you be bold if you don't know what type of business you're in?

YOU ARE GIFTED

Human beings are fascinated by what we deem "extraordinary" abilities, talents that some people seem to naturally possess. Things that impress us. The truth is we are all talented in our own ways. What's important is understanding what it is that you are talented at. I truly believe that each of you were handcrafted for a purpose that only you can fulfill. Discovering that purpose, however, can take time.

I've been in church services where the message implied, "If you don't act now, God will use someone else." Every time I think about it, I cringe because God can certainly get the job done with or without us. That's not the point. The point is if God wants us—you personally—to accomplish something, we will. But shouldn't there be a key element of motivation? Shouldn't we be inspired to make a contribution in our lifetime without feeling pressured to?

Your gifts will come under attack. If you're going to grow in your career, there are reviews and criticism that might be uncomfortable to hear but are meant to be communicated with you in a safe place. On the other hand, there are also people who want you to feel a burn from their words and criticism.

What do you do when someone uses their words as a weapon? When someone might be putting unfair pressure on you? In some cases, even setting the standard so high you will never match up?

Dealing with these situations leaves you questioning your gifts. It is a lonely place. You wonder if the critics were right. Was I living a lie?

So I called an old friend, someone I'd worked with in the past. I could hear his anger over the phone. He told me, "We can all learn from a healthy critic, but you must protect your heart from true attacks." He would inspire me to stop letting it take up emotional space.

So what does this mean? Does finding your gift put a target on your back? Yes, it does. So you need to be prepared to defend not only yourself but your abilities.

LEARN HOW TO PROTECT YOUR GIFT
First, Check the Source

My freshmen year of college I struggled with sarcasm. I came from a community that didn't use sarcasm as humor. Our humor came from shock value. So attending a college where I was surrounded by people who have perfected sarcasm meant I was angry a lot. I felt like I was being bullied. Finally, I went to my friend, and he said, "Check the source."

What does this mean? This means that everybody doesn't get a free access card to your life. There are people you have to rule out because they aren't cheering for your success. They are actually waiting for you to fail.

Barring people from your life doesn't come easily. I often give more chances than I ought to. It stems from my need for grace. There were people who believed in me when I was at my worst. To this day, I am thankful for that. So how do you show grace while not exposing yourself to harm? It's complicated.

Shutting people out without speaking with them first is not a bold move. Having a conversation is. There are people who won't realize they're creating a problem until you point it out. Yes, it can be uncomfortable. Most of us don't enjoy conflict, but it can be a necessary step in protecting your gift without cutting everyone out of your life.

On the other hand, there are people who have already made their minds up about you, and no amount of talking will change them. They aren't going to change or respect your leadership. In cases like this, an appropriate dismissal is acceptable.

The truly scary part is when this applies to family. Family is for life. So how do you get a family member to change their attitude toward you? How do you get someone who you want in your life to start respecting you? It comes down to time. Patience. Grace.

Of course, there are always exceptions to every rule. Even family. Instances of abuse, addiction, even mental health issues complicate things. By no means will I tell you your bold journey will be easy. It won't be.

In order to deal with this source, you have to be ready for some extremely gracious days. Your grace for your family member will have to be as big as the universe. Be prepared to be bold. Set boundaries and keep them!

Second, Strengthen Your Gift

I once encountered a man who was extremely talented. He was an impressively quick learner. Taught himself to do almost anything by simply watching videos. His friends told me he'd learned to play piano by watching it on the computer. He was a likeable man, and his friends enjoyed his company. But what he had in talent he lacked in follow through.

He never completed anything he started. He dropped out of school and lied about it for months. His IQ must have been off the charts, but he simply never bothered to strengthen this amazing gift he'd been given.

Strengthening your gifts means being willing to continually learn and grow. Never giving up in the face of harsh criticism. Your critics can't decide for you if you'll accomplish your dreams. They'll be too busy cleaning from their glasses all the dust you've left them in.

Strengthen your gift by learning, practicing, and letting your mistakes make you better. Treat your destiny like the big game and each day as though it's practice.

Third, Remove the Clutter

In this day and age, there's more clutter in our lives than ever before. We have instant access to whatever we want. Endless distractions. Every minute of your day can be drowned by clutter. There has to be a set time for that clutter to be swept away. And I'm not just talking about technology. We all have different temptations just waiting to clutter our lives.

One afternoon I asked a man I knew if he wanted to go golfing and clear his mind. He looked at me like he'd seen a ghost and said, "Never! My father destroyed my family because he was addicted to golfing."

For that man, golf was clutter.

From sports to hobbies, anything that consumes you to the point that your relationships and career suffer is clutter. It's a form of addiction.

I'm not saying that we should all stop doing things we enjoy. Of course not. But if you cannot detach yourself from these things, there's a clutter situation. Sometimes these situations aren't even apparent to us. We don't realize we've become addicted to something beyond the point of healthy enjoyment. If you listen to the people around you, you might better identify your clutter.

I use the word *clutter* instead of *addiction* because clutter can be fixed quickly. When my kids are playing and there's stuff everywhere, it becomes difficult for them to focus on a single toy. But cleanup is quick and simple, and it can make all the difference.

Fourth, Set Deadlines

Deadlines can be a major cause for anxiety, a clock constantly ticking away in the back of your mind. But sometimes they are necessary, and the result is worth it.

I don't like deadlines, and I really wish I didn't have to deal with them. I said it; thank you for letting me be honest. But I do like having things done on time. I like knowing that people will see me as responsible if I am able to meet a deadline. What does this have to do with my gift?

In the business world, deadlines become the pot of gold at the end of the rainbow. This is where the money is made. By setting a deadline, you make it clear that the result is important to you.

However, there are times when deadlines aren't met. Goals aren't accomplished in a set amount of time. This can be frustrating and embarrassing, so be realistic. Take time to organize your calendar. I'd love to sound highly religious here and remind you to mark time for God on your schedule, but that would defeat the purpose of allowing God to be present in everything you do.

Your calendar should help you clearly see your deadlines. It should give you an opportunity to remove clutter from your schedule and help you make better decisions about how to manage your time. Hearing stories from people I've advised to make changes to their personal calendar has been exciting.

I've spoken with people going through divorces and seen their lives change when they revamp their calendars. I've met students who dropped out of high school and witnessed them find the motivation to finish. I've watched broken families piece themselves back together. I met a man once who was struggling to start his own business, and when I asked him to show me his calendar, he couldn't. He didn't have one. Once he put together a calendar, he was able to double his profits just by seeing his week from a broader perspective.

You might be thinking, *Easier said than done.* You're right! It takes boldness to really see what you do for business in light of your calling. The book of Proverbs reveals a way to allow everything we do to reap success: "Commit everything you do to the Lord. Trust him to help you do it and he will" (Proverbs 37:5 TLB).

You have to crawl before you walk. I encourage you to start small. Set small deadlines, and build your confidence. Trust God to increase your boldness so that you can bring the bold you anywhere you go.

THE KING'S BUSINESS (DANIEL 8)

Have you ever had a dream that you just couldn't shake? We all have, including Daniel. In the last verse of chapter 8, it says that he got up and still went about the king's business, even while feeling overwhelmed.

As I read this chapter and the different landmarks mentioned in it, I was fascinated by the fact that they were sophisticated enough to know about such faraway places as Greece. Had they seen pictures? Heard stories from travelers?

Daniel lived his life in utter trust of God, and the knowledge of

God was given to him as he slept. Visions of war and carnage that would have troubled anyone. Imagine having vivid dreams of World War II. Just looking at old footage is enough to turn my stomach.

But what Daniel saw wasn't in the past. They were images of a coming war. Horrors and devastation that they had yet to face. And there was nothing Daniel could do except hold on to it. No earthly army of his day could prevent the destruction he saw. Only God could intervene.

ARE YOU ABOUT THE KING'S BUSINESS?

I have met a lot of people who are convinced that God doesn't accept them anymore because they have been living in sin. They are afraid that because they have been part of various activities, they aren't even welcome in the church. As crazy as I think they sound, I know exactly how they feel.

If you have experienced this, you are someone who leans toward wanting to be part of the king's business. You're not meant to live wildly for the world but to be relentless about the king's business.

Rebellion

When your angry rebellion feels good. Telling off your boss, relative, or even a stranger when they cross you gives you a sense of power. Being able to do what you want when you want; it's freedom. Isn't it? It makes you feel invincible. And in these invincible moments, it becomes really easy to tell people to stay out of your business. I've been there.

When I walked through my seasons of rebellion, I wanted my business to be my own. But that sense of freedom and power it gives you is false. The longer I rebelled, the lonelier I felt. I wasn't being filled by the king's business.

My mind and heart gave into the flesh. My thoughts and language became explicit and unfiltered. There was nothing to hide. Until I surrendered to God's business I could no longer break this cycle.

I pray my transparency will be an illustration of what happens when we allow God to transform our minds. Recognize that thoughts and speech go together with your business. If you don't think like a hero, you will never speak or act like one.

Boundaries

Setting clear boundaries is key to boldness. Your boundaries reveal your values, and your values reveal your character. Boundaries need to be clearly defined for your friends, family, relationships, and employers.

We can all look back and pinpoint situations where having set boundaries could have saved us undue stress. Setting boundaries doesn't steal your freedom to be bold. It gives you the space you need to be just that.

However, boundaries can be abused. I've met people who are so strict about their boundaries that it causes others to be uncomfortable around them. I had a friend who chose to become a vegan. Mealtimes with her were always tense. "How can you eat that?" she'd ask, accusingly. "It used to be alive? I don't eat anything that had a face."

Jokingly, I'd respond, "What about your salad? What about *Veggie Tales*?" This made her laugh. I continued to eat my chicken sandwich.

So how do we set boundaries without appearing to be the religious Pharisee or the helicopter mom? We cannot just enforce the boundaries and when they aren't understood say, "Because I said so," or ask, "Why should I have to explain myself?" This doesn't build a community. It becomes more of an elephant in the room.

First, are your boundaries a personal preference? Are they meant for you? Can you still function in a group or social environment without them becoming completely shattered?

Second, do you have boundaries for everything? If you have found you're on the search for control, you may be using your boundaries as a way to gain control over your life. It will be good for you to start learning how to remain confident without imposing unfair standards on others. This is tricky. This deserves deep thought. Are you still living boldly yet keeping your standards?

Third, have an explanation. Use your knowledge as a way to reveal how the research you have done has helped you and shaped your conclusion. This will continue to keep the lines of communication open, and at the same time, help you to see where you can show grace when others don't understand.

Fourth, be a continual learner. Learning what differences exist are important. This can actually strengthen your fundamental beliefs. If you were to travel to a different country, you would not expect them to understand your customs. It would be silly to demand a classroom in the Ukraine to say the Pledge of Allegiance to the United States because you have entered the room. Each person you meet is completely different from you. Our biggest influence isn't setting unfair standards; it comes through radical understanding.

Boldness is not an incognito way of giving out free passes to be a bully. Boldness is your free pass to be a world changer. Your hero status will be gravely affected if you become known as a bully. Take time to be teachable, and learn how to inspire others through your boldness.

Big Business

Your life, desires, and dreams are big business. You get one chance here on earth to accomplish what you can. You may leave a big mark or a little one, but whatever it is, we needed it! We need you! Your contribution is big business. I'm glad you're part of the journey.

CHALLENGE: DREAM

You're allowed to dream. You're allowed to pray. You're even allowed to want success in your life without feeling selfish. It your dreams have been given to you by God, seek wisdom then run full speed ahead!

Take an opportunity to think about your dreams. Take time to make God's business your business. Take a moment to step back into your hero status and be bolder than ever!

Chapter 9

BATTLEFIELD OF BOLDNESS

For our struggle is not against flesh and blood, but against the
rulers, against the authorities, against the powers of this dark world
and against the spiritual forces of evil in the heavenly realms.
—Ephesians 6:12 (NIV)

"Only eight dollars?"

The ATM was only a short drive from my house, but I was on pins
and needles the entire way. A few unexpected expenses had me on edge,
and I dreaded that "Remaining Balance" screen. Cruising around the
side of the bank, I slid my card into the machine and keyed in the pin
number.

"Do you want to print your balance?"

No. No, I did not.

I hit yes.

The ATM whirred and hummed and spit out a seemingly harmless
slip of paper. And it wasn't the paper that sent my anxiety skyrocketing.
It was the little numbers printed on it.

"Only eight dollars?" I had to stop for a moment and close my eyes.
I took a deep breath, pocketed the receipt, put the car in drive, and
drove home.

Doubt plagued me the entire way. I wasn't getting paid enough.

Why was I even in ministry? Obviously not for the money, but was helping people and being broke all the time worth it?

When I got home, my wife could immediately tell something was wrong. She followed me into the bedroom, where I took off my shoes, threw them across the room, and flopped onto my back on the bed.

"What's the matter?" she wanted to know.

What wasn't the matter? "Everything," I told her. "We can't even afford to buy groceries this week."

We were out of food, and it was only Saturday. Thursday was a long way off. One of the things I love most about my wife is her ability to remain calm while I panic. She let me lie there and then told me, "We'll make it work."

She sat there with me, and before she left the room, we prayed together. Prayer brought me some peace, but the lack of funds still nagged the back of my mind.

The next morning, we left for church, where I served as a youth pastor. It was in the country, so our drive consisted of farms, fields, and the occasional Amish buggy. Not much to distract me from the thoughts souring my mind. I struggled the whole way to get my head straight, so I could be of value to those kids and their families.

As the service came to an end, one of the men in the congregation came over to Jennifer and shook her hand. When he pulled back there was cash in her palm. She looked at me, and I just knew it was an answer to our prayers. That gentle handshake provided us enough to buy groceries for the rest of the week.

I learned a huge lesson that day. It's during the battles that our boldness must be on the frontlines.

FRONTLINE

I've spoken with many men and women who have served in the military. I always ask them about their time in boot camp. About their drill sergeants. And their answers are always the same. "At first it was hard, but once we realized they were breaking us down so we could be built up, it actually made sense."

The drill sergeants were in their ears and got into their heads to save their lives. Once the solider could focus while being screamed at, he or she could focus under any amount of pressure on the battlefield.

We often resent the idea of being on the frontlines because the stress of it causes discomfort. But the situations we face that force us outside our comfort zones are actually opportunities. You are being shaped with patience.

It's amazing to look back over all that you have survived. And to foresee all that you will survive because you've allowed those opportunities to educate you.

WHAT IS YOUR BATTLEFIELD?

Everybody has a different battlefield. For some of us, finances are our biggest struggle. We're afraid to look at our available balances. Afraid to ask for help. Our checkbooks are a mess, and so are we because we define our value by a number on a screen rather than by God's unlimited love. Overdue bills become blinders to our greatest blessings.

For others, our children can be our battlefields. If you have children who are particularly challenging or possess special needs, they can consume your mind. You want them to grow up as normally as possible, and any differences become stressful and difficult to shake.

Relationships can be another kind of battlefield. Some people are in love with the idea of being in love. The desire to be in a relationship is all-consuming. It can lead to jealousy and trust issues. We put so much weight on our value as a part of a relationship that we forget about our value as a whole in God's love.

For some people, self-esteem is difficult. Even the smallest things can trigger self-doubt. A series of unfortunate events has you at your wit's end, and you just cannot take another hang up.

And there are others. Other struggles. Other battles we all face. So many others. Every person is different, but in each scenario, the antidote is the same: value. Finding the right things to place value on can help anyone live a good life.

Now, a good life doesn't mean no more struggles. It doesn't mean your bills will be magically paid or Prince Charming will walk through your front door. It simply means that you will find a way to overcome those struggles. And that makes you bolder than ever!

FAITH

Faith is a gift of God. God gives us the opportunity to partner with Him when it concerns faith. Sin, pain, sickness and all trials try to nullify faith by stealing this gift. Based on 1 Peter 1:6-7, our faith is refined and we are strengthened and even purified by like gold through the trials. Jesus broke the curse. You are free.

Before I was diagnosed with lupus, I had all sorts of issues. My fingers would stop working, and I would get sick. I was afraid to talk about it. I was speaking and teaching about the power of God all the time. What would people think if the preacher needed to be healed?

It got to the point that I avoided some people because I felt like I was being judged. Did I not have enough faith? Was I a failure at rebuking the sickness in my body? It became a serious insecurity for me.

Finally, one evening my church had a prayer walk. I hadn't told anybody about my disease at this point out of fear for my job. There were many stations along the walk. Each station focused on God's greatness. At the last station, you could receive prayer.

I knew what each of the stations were ahead of time, so once I saw that nobody was at the prayer station, I approached it. My emotions immediately got the best of me. I told the man standing there, offering prayer, about my disease. "I have lupus." When the words passed my lips, something inside me broke. I didn't claim to be strong. I'd already accepted all that this horrible disease entails. I brought it to a fight. From this point on I stopped claiming the illness as "my or mine." Nothing about this cruel mystery belonged to my hero status. Jesus won the battle and from this point forward I was going to battle from a place of victory. I sought prayer often and even on my worst days I never backed down.

Imagine taking your problems to God is like dragging them into a fistfight. The issues that have bullied and controlled you for years are ready for a beatdown. By confessing through prayer what plagues you, you are preparing yourself to defeat it.

After we prayed, I met many other people with problems of their own. Because I'd brought my problem into prayer, I was prepared to face it and help others face theirs.

FAITH HALL OF FAME

Who in your life have demonstrated superior faith? It's always good to identify these people and learn from them. Let their faith be your guide for it may be your faith that guides others. Faith is contagious!

Whenever I have the opportunity to hear a speaker tell a story about an example of superior faith, I always find myself inspired. I want to live my life on a new faith level. I become recommitted to finding ways to show and share my faith with others.

The author of Hebrews wrote a list in chapter 11 of people from the Old Testament who made a profound difference through faith. Chapter 11 starts out with a definition of faith. It states, "Now, faith is being sure of what we hope for and certain of what we do not see" (Hebrews 11:1 NIV). As I read through the different names, I remind myself of their lives. They had no instant technology. They relied 100 percent on God. He uses the phrase, "By faith," to explain each of their accomplishments through God's will.

"By faith, Abraham" (Hebrews 11:17 NIV).
"By faith, Jacob" (Hebrews 11:21 NIV).
"By faith, Moses" (Hebrews 11:25 NIV).

The inspiration behind this is very simple. What will you accomplish by faith? Taking time to trust God with the direction of your life, and hold on to His faithfulness during your journey. God knows your future, and He is guiding you, loving you, holding you despite the mistakes you might make. You belong to Him, and it's time to trust.

Write your name on the lines below.

By faith, _____ made a difference at his/her workplace.

By faith, _____ showed compassion for the poor.
By faith, _____ made a lasting difference in his/her family.

God isn't calling you to get dizzy watching the world spin. He has called you to be a light in the darkness. Rise up and be bold as His kingdom is built, and the walls of the enemy begin to crumble. He's called you to go above and beyond. Now is your time to share the good news and accomplish great things. There is no such thing as passive faith. There is only passionate faith. We don't sit around hoping we get on our feet and watch it happen.

Don't let humility become pride. You've been placed in this corner of the earth for a purpose. God knew exactly where you would be before you ever did.

Are you comfortable? Angry? Do you feel betrayed? Brokenhearted? Do you think the problems you face are too big for God? They're not. God is big enough to know the cry of your heart. But are you brave enough to place them in His hands and say yes to the calling He has placed on your life?

Let's remember Jesus has "Savior status," but in Christ, you will have a hero status Being a hero doesn't make you prideful. It means you are willing to persevere. You are willing to help others. You aren't just some robot, running on autopilot day in and day out. You wake up each morning, praying for the opportunity to help others.

Are You in the Hall of Fame?

There's something inspiring about walking through the section of the Baseball Hall of Fame dedicated to Babe Ruth. He's a legend. His ability to hit a baseball mesmerized the world.

When you enter the hall, the first thing you see is a picture of him. I always have to stop and look because you can see it there in his eyes … the soul of a man who did not give up. He never allowed his past to stop him from swinging a baseball bat and hitting home runs. He didn't let it stop him from becoming a hero to millions of people.

I'm not handing out participation trophies here. I'm not giving you a free pass just for trying. This chapter is about accomplishing the hard things. It's about becoming great. In life, you don't get anything unless you give it your all. If you want to be in the hall of fame, you need to hit home runs. You need to help your team win. You need to be bold! You need to change your status.

Are you working your way toward the hall of fame, or did you only buy a ticket to the game? Are you willing to work harder? Are you willing to learn to communicate better? Are you willing to dream bigger? This is what decides your status. This is where you decide how the battle is going to play out.

Don't wait until your family starts falling apart before you make the first move. Don't wait until finals to start studying. The moment your feet hit the ground, dig deep. The battle has already begun.

DANIEL'S WAR (DANIEL 9)

The war Daniel fought was against sin. Sin was the enemy, and the enemy had invaded the people. It was winning. But everything inside Daniel wanted to be right before God.

One reason was God's promise that He would not allow the captives to return home for at least seventy years. Daniel fully understood this, but he wanted nothing more than to go home. He wanted to be in his own land, away from the angst created by being in the palace of a tyrant king.

Daniel trusted in God's blessing, and as we've read throughout this book, he always kept a level head. Sometimes, I wonder what his bad days were like. We all have them. Did Daniel get frustrated? Did he ever want to give up? He must have. But we don't read about these bad days. We read about a man who never stopped fighting, despite bad days. We read about a man who gave his new land a run for its money. Daniel pushed forward and persevered. If there was a war, he was never on the losing side.

As you read Daniel's prayer, it's clear what he believes about his battle. Daniel doesn't pray in fear. He prays with the passion to fight.

Now, our God, hear the prayers and petitions of your servant.
For your sake, Lord, look with favor on your desolate sanctuary.
Give ear, our God, and hear; open your eyes and see the
desolation of the city that bears your Name. We do not make
requests of you because we are righteous, but because of your
great mercy. Lord, listen! Lord, forgive! Lord, hear and act!
For your sake, my God, do not delay, because your city and
your people bear your Name. (Daniel 9:17–19 NIV)

Everything about the battle before you is meant to reveal God's faithfulness. In some of life's terrible moments, you can feel like your grief and anger cannot be penetrated. But it's during these battles that you reveal how bold you really are. Battles aren't caused by failure; they're opportunities to commit yourself to being faithful.

NEVER BACK DOWN

Never allow anyone to steal your joy. There is a chain reaction. The Holy Spirit fuels your joy and joy fuels your boldness. You cannot be bold if your tank is empty. You need a reason to fight. Overcoming darkness is impossible without any light.

There have been a few seasons in my life when I had enough. Where it felt like my tank was nearing the E. It was during these times that I questioned my goals in life. I didn't want to be a good person; being angry was just easier. No more Mr. Nice Guy.

I found myself not wanting to be around people who encouraged me. I wanted to be left alone until I could figure things out for myself. I made sure that the people mistaking my kindness for weakness were put in their places. Yet, amid this turmoil, I could always feel God's presence.

He was always with me, encouraging me not to continue in my outrage and leading me to learn humility. I had to accept that my strength was never meant to be in that type of aggression but in the righteousness stored in my heart.

As I prayed one day, I felt God challenge me: "They might have hurt you, but I didn't. They might have let you go, but I will hold on to you forever. You're not done!"

Never back down from being the person God made you to be. Never let go of your joy. You are not done!

CHALLENGE: SELF-ESTEEM

Look back at every time you've been tempted to give up and remind yourself:

I am not done!
I will keep fighting for joy!
I will keep fighting for value!
I will keep fighting for righteousness!
I am bolder than ever!

Chapter 10

BREATHE BOLDLY

*I consider my life worth nothing to me; my only aim is to
finish the race and complete the task the Lord Jesus has given
me—the task of testifying to the good news of God's grace.*
—Acts 20:24 (NIV)

"Because every little thing will be all right."

It was still dark outside when I woke because my stomach felt weird. Careful not to wake my wife, Jennifer, I slipped out of our room and checked on our daughter as she slept before heading into work early. I tried everything I could think of to shake this awkward feeling, but nothing worked. As the day passed, it only grew, so I called my wife and told her I was coming home. She asked what was wrong, and I told her I wasn't feeling well.

"Haven't you been eating a lot of jalapeños lately?" she asked. I had to laugh. I do love my spicy food.

When I arrived home, I crawled into bed and slept until she had to go to work. I was still exhausted and experiencing a lot of pain, but she only needed to work for a few hours, so I got up to take care of our six-month-old little girl.

Making sure she was changed, fed, and happy depleted what little strength I had left until I found myself too weak to even walk. I kept looking at the clock, waiting for Jennifer's shift to end. Finally, I texted her, "I have to go to urgent care." What I should have said was, "I have to go to the emergency room."

Jennifer quickly made sure our daughter had everything she needed and put her in the car. She even had to help get me in the car. When we arrived at urgent care, the doctor explained my appendix was rupturing, and I needed to go straight to the emergency room. There I was given pain medication and scheduled for surgery the following morning.

The surgery went fine, but waking from the anesthesia was a battle. I couldn't seem to catch my breath and kept slipping into this dreamy state. I didn't want to escape from it. But then there were voices calling to me. Hands shaking me. An oxygen mask was placed over my face.

I had to fight to breathe. Every gasp hurt, but with each breath, I grew more and more alert.

I'll never forget the sound of those nurses calling my name. "Joe! You have to wake up! Come on, Joe! Wake up!"

Their voices faded in and out as I struggled to regain consciousness. I was wheeled from one recovery room to another and lost all track of time. I had no idea how long I fought to breathe before I finally succeeded.

When Jennifer came into the room, I knew it must have been bad. The look on her face … I could see how scared she was. I was still very weak. Talking was difficult, but the last thing I wanted was for my wife to be afraid, so I tried to sing to her from under the oxygen mask.

For whatever reason, I chose the song "Three Little Birds" by Bob Marley. It may have sounded like a whisper, and the only line of the song I could get out was, "Don't worry about a thing because every little thing is going to be all right."

She was smiling and crying all at the same time, and I couldn't have been prouder. She held it together and took care of our baby girl while I faced a medical emergency.

ON THE OTHER SIDE OF THE BED

I've visited hundreds of people in the hospital. I've learned proper visitor etiquette and to let the patient run the show. Some will talk your ear off for an hour or more, while others just want to see your face.

Hospital visits can be very unpredictable. I admire doctors and nurses who work there every day. They face a side of life daily that the rest of us only glimpse and then try to forget.

Our faith journey can be a lot like a hospital visit. Sometimes we're the patients in need of someone to share their testimony with. The sick in need of a savior. Other times, we're the visitors. I take every opportunity I'm given to play this role. I've spoken with people in government, medical professionals, teachers, and many more from all areas of life.

Who will share the light of life if we don't? Who will care about people who are broken if we don't? Why does the spirit of judgment interfere with the work of Christ?

What side of the bed are you on? Are you a patient in need of medical attention or the friend or loved one sitting in the bedside chair? These questions can be the motivation we need to share the love of Christ. But they can also cause a lot of pressure. Maybe you don't feel ready. Maybe you don't think you're qualified to spread God's Word.

Think about it. Who first shared his or her faith with you? Was the individual a professional? A "God expert?" Does such a thing even exist? Did the person have all the answers? I doubt it. But in some way, that conversation opened your heart and allowed the breath of salvation to fill your soul.

I believe you are qualified!

HEALING WORDS

Healing is part of the redemptive work of Jesus. Healing is something that we can claim. It doesn't mean that you won't get sick. It means you can rebuke sickness and claim healing. But sometimes things don't work out the way we expect them to.

I've asked many times, "What if I rebuke sickness, and the person stays sick? What if I'm sick, and I'm not getting better?"

They are difficult questions to wrestle with and can even become strongholds for nonbelievers. They want to know why God didn't heal their mothers or why their children had to die?

When faced with these answerless questions, I hang on to the passage where Jesus says, "Ask and it will be given to you; seek and you will find; knock and the door will be opened to you" (Matthew 7:7 NIV).

There is a temptation to say, "God didn't heal me," or, "I prayed, and nothing happened." These words create doubt. Jesus paid the debt, we get to claim healing, we are freed from the prison. Unbelief cannot be accepted. In fact, if you are experiencing sickness, it is in these moments when fixing your eyes on Jesus will be the great reminder that you are healed. According to Matthew 8:14–17, as Jesus is healing the sick and casting out demons, there is a passage from Isaiah that is quoted. It states, "He took up our infirmities and carried our diseases" (Matthew 8:17 NIV). We are freed from sickness, and our eyes must now remain fixed on Jesus. He paid the price of sin for all of us once and for all! The boldest prayer you can pray is one that claims your freedom from sin and sickness!

When we look at the book of James, it is revealed that "He chose to give us birth through the word of truth, that we might be a kind of first-fruits of all he created" (James 1:7–8 NIV).

The qualification is in place. The debt was paid. You have already been set free. Embrace this freedom! The word of truth gave you life, and the word of truth can be passed on by you. You can speak and live boldly because God picked you!

Speech Development

Language is fluid, constantly changing, which can make communication complicated. There are slang words that are acceptable in some areas and offensive in others. Times and places for certain topics of conversation. Religion has even become one of those "right place, right time" topics.

I've learned speech development is something that cannot be ignored. There are so many components to speech: the ability to hear, repeat, and express. When a child has a hard time with any of these, he or she may need to work with a speech therapist to the problem and learn to communicate more clearly.

When it comes to our personal boldness, are we able to listen, repeat, and express? Are we intentional about our calling to speak life, hear life, and share life? Struggling with one of these areas isn't the problem. The problem lies with our motivation and the passion behind it.

The book of James reveals a very interesting passage about problems. First, you count it as pure joy. That may seem strange, but joy comes from having identified a problem that can now be fixed. Then, as you seek to understand and learn, you are led farther along in your faith journey. And lastly, by overcoming the struggle, you will receive a crown of life. This is a promise (James 1:1–12).

Taking time to develop your speech is an exciting investment. The process sets you up to be highly effective and provides insight when you are called to share the true nature of the gospel with someone in desperate need of a savior.

BOUNDARIES THE SEQUEL

The first time I worked in construction, I found myself surrounded by men with no verbal filter. Their word choices often turned vulgar at the flip of a switch, and it wasn't long before I found their words creeping into my vocabulary.

I'd worked hard to clean up my language, but now—spending forty hours a week surrounded by men who didn't even notice how profanity slipped into every sentence they spoke—I struggled to keep it that way. It was almost like a language all their own, and the best way to become fluent in any language is to immerse yourself in it.

The book of James states, "The tongue also is a fire, it corrupts the whole person, sets the whole course of his life on fire, and is itself set on fire by hell" (James 3:6 NIV).

I want to accompany this verse with 2 Timothy 2:16 (NIV): "Avoid godless chatter, because those who indulge in it will become more and more ungodly."

Creating boundaries will help you remain confident in your boldness.

First, cleanse your mind and heart. Your words come from what you feel and what you know. Therefore, what you feel and what you know need a checkup. Take time to think about righteousness, and exclude those words and conversations from the process.

Second, look closely at what entertains you, and do an overhaul. Our society pays big bucks to hear crude comedians and is then shocked to hear a political figure use the same language. The standards are equal, so we must seek encouraging entertainment that will not taint other areas of our lives.

Third, know when to tune out and tune in. In the workplace, and sometimes even with particular friends, we must choose to tune out certain aspects of their speech. In other situations, you may find an opportunity to be brave and share the gospel.

RESTLESS

One evening I saw the perfect image of restlessness. I watched a video of the "pool of death," which is located in East Kauai, Hawaii. In the video, three young men jumped in the water, and the current kept swirling around them. The tide came in and out. The men would reach for the cliff and try to catch their breath. But as soon as they got close, the tide pulled them off of the wall, and they would fight the current again.

Spiritually speaking, restlessness is a sign we are looking for something to cling to in our swirling environments. This doesn't reveal weakness. I believe it reveals your strength. Overcoming your different bouts with restlessness prepares you to remain confident in the stillness and ready to fight when things seem to be uncertain.

Feeling restless isn't a punishment. Restlessness is a reminder that your situation requires you to hold on to the peace of God. The peace of God comes from the presence of the Holy Spirit and the Word of God. The Word of God transforms your restlessness from recklessness to righteousness. You can take that righteousness and apply it to your employment, relationships, health, children, and other tensions.

Restlessness stirs up boldness. When you are restless, you do things you wouldn't do if you were calm. Restlessness releases your inner hero. You are fighting to cling to solid ground. You are fighting for stability. You are fighting to make a change. Every hero has a moment when one realizes he or she is driven by some type of restlessness. You were born to be a difference maker!

DANIEL 10: I CAN HARDLY BREATHE

When it comes to Daniel chapters 10–12, we must keep in mind they are prophetic. These chapters are revealing the power of God's foreknowledge. I want to clearly make the point that my goal is to draw out moments that pertain to this book's theme, which is boldness—drawing out our inner heroes. It's these moments that give us the courage to face new challenges and get past old ones.

Daniel chapter 10 reveals a conversation he has with one he refers to as "one who looked like a man" (Daniel 10:16 NIV). Up to this moment, it reveals only that Daniel heard the prophetic word that was brought to him. The men with him fled and were terrified, leaving Daniel standing alone.

Daniel was terrified. He admits in verse 17, "My strength is gone and I can hardly breathe" (Daniel 10:17 NIV). This reveals the very human side to Daniel. He was facing danger. He was facing a power greater than his own. Sometimes when we are truly frightened, catching our breath is a sign that our fear has completely overwhelmed us.

The theme of this chapter reveals breath and breathing as examples of strength. Strength should always coexist with boldness. So when I look at Daniel 10: 18 (NIV), the man spoke strength over Daniel.

Again the one who looked like a man touched me and gave me strength. "Do not be afraid, you who are highly esteemed," he said. "Peace! Be strong now; be strong." When he spoke to me, I was strengthened and said, "Speak, my lord, since you have given me strength." (Daniel 10:18–19 NIV)

The Word of God has the ability to cause us to tremble and give us strength. God's Word breathes life, and when God spoke to the formless world, it came to be. If God can speak in you, the Word can transform what you believe to be failure and guide you into a fearless future!

NEVER STOP SPEAKING

The Word of God is powerful. "All-scripture is God-breathed and is useful for teaching, rebuking, correcting and training in righteousness" (2 Timothy 3:16 NIV).

If we meditate on the Word of God and use it and speak it, are we speaking the breath of God? Is there life in our speech? I would like to believe that when I share the Word of God with someone, I am sharing the breath of God. I am sharing life!

For many of us, this next question is going to be challenging or affirming. If the Spirit of God left you, would you know the difference? I want to be so full of God's Word and filled with the Holy Spirit that if it ever left me, I would know instantly. My prayer is for God to never stop speaking to me. I cannot do it by myself.

CHALLENGE: ABIDE

Would your life change if the Spirit of God left you? Could you still accomplish everything you have to do? Would you sense it and become restless? God is calling us to abide in Him.

When we abide in Christ we exchange complacency for confidence, pride for promises, and rebellion for righteousness. You are no longer helpless but stand boldly as a hero.

Chapter 11

BELIEVABLE BOLDNESS

*The people went out to see what had happened. When
they came to Jesus, they found the man from whom
the demons had gone out, sitting at Jesus' feet, dressed
and in his right mind; and they were afraid.*
—Luke 8:35 (NIV)

"I have to run after him!"

During the summer of 2004, I had the pleasure of spending some time with a traveling evangelism team. I traveled by train from Syracuse, New York, to Racine, Wisconsin, and from there, we hit the road. It was fantastic.

Our goal was to teach churches a better, bolder approach to sharing the love of Christ in their communities. It was a lot of work but well worth the effort. Seeing some of the shiest people I've ever met come back and tell us they were finally able to speak with a neighbor or friend about their faith was inspiring.

After being on the road for about a month, we found ourselves in a small town south of Minneapolis. Mornings there were humid, and all night long we served as an all-you-can-eat buffet for the thriving mosquito population. Despite that, we were having a great week, meeting lots of people from the local church, and building strong bonds between team members.

One day I was walking along the street with a fellow teammate when I spotted a man coming in our direction. He was walking quickly, and something about him just felt … off. Talking with strangers has never been a problem for me. In fact, no matter where I am or who I'm with, if I believe God is speaking to me about something, I do everything in my power to follow through. And in that moment, I felt a call to speak with that man.

I stopped and said, "Hey, bro, can I talk to you?" It was clear from the way he shifted from foot to foot and kept glancing down the street that he was on edge. He looked ready to flee, so I launched right into a conversation. As I explained how Jesus had rescued me, he began to settle. I told him that Jesus could do the same for him.

Something changed then. The man looked at me and said, "I need that. I'm in a weird spot. I need help. I really needed to hear that today."

As soon as he had finished, he continued on his way, moving quickly down the sidewalk. It wasn't until he was out of sight that I realized I'd forgotten to give him a Bible. The part of me that knows running is not my thing wanted to let it go, but my heart said otherwise. I looked at my teammate and told her, "I have to run after him!"

I ran for nearly seven blocks before I caught up with him, huffing and puffing as I held the book in my hands. "Did you run after me just to give me a Bible?" he asked.

I told him that I had and that God had put words on my heart to share with him. I told him, "You might be going through a difficult time in your life right now. It might feel like you've burned every bridge in your life, but you're loved and forgiven. Trust Jesus in your journey. You are my brother."

The blood drained from the man's face. He looked like he'd just seen a ghost when he said, "Yo, for real man. I believe you. I need Jesus right now in my life. I have a lot going on." I asked him if I could pray for him one more time, and he agreed.

By the time I got back to my teammate, I was drenched with sweat. The whole ride back to the church I had my window down, trying to dry out my shirt with no luck. When we arrived, the others laughed and asked, "Joe, what happened? This is going to be a good one." So I shared the story of what happened.

The next morning, I joined the pastor and his wife for breakfast. She held a newspaper, and when I came to the table, she told me, "You weren't alone yesterday."

Sure enough, the headline read, "Escaped Criminal." And there, just below the byline, was the image of a face I immediately recognized. He'd faked an injury and escaped from the hospital. No wonder he'd looked so desperate. He was in serious trouble. And even though I hadn't known at the time, God did. In the midst of his desperation, God used me—an average person—to chase him and reveal the boldness of Jesus.

THE CHASE

What are you chasing? I've met people chasing love, people chasing money, even people chasing adventure. People chase all sorts of things. And then I've met people who are so busy they aren't really chasing anything. They're simply running in circles.

Some people chase goals like retirement, financial stability, and a bigger house. But is that it? There is an array of goals to chase. If you think through what is important to you and what should be important to you, you will understand why you think the way you do. Self-centered, Short-term, and short-lived? Is that the best we can aim for? What about leaving a legacy? What about making a significant contribution to the world? What about living with a purpose? Is your chase about keeping up with the latest trends? Or about being a trendsetter? Do you want to be like everyone else? What are you teaching your children? To be like everyone else or to be confident in their individuality?

I remember when Starter jackets first came out. Such a huge fad. If you don't know what they are, you should Google "Starter Jackets." I just had to have a Charlotte Hornets jacket. I didn't follow basketball, and I had an irrational fear of bees, but I liked the colors and wanted to have it before anyone else in my class did. Within three months, a wide variety of team jackets were being worn by every last person in the classroom, and most of us couldn't name three players on the team. We wore them simply because everyone else did.

Things like Starter jackets come with unrealistic expectations: that we'll make more friends, become more popular, and that people will think more highly of us. It's completely untrue. So with all the shiny, flashy things in this world, how do we know what's worth chasing?

First off, stop chasing everything at once. It's important to have focus. Know the difference between hobbies, passions, and gifts.

One day I got a flat tire on my bike, so I took it to a bike shop. I got to talking with the man behind the counter, and he confided that he'd, "ruined a great hobby." He'd taken his love of bikes and opened a bike shop. Years later, he resented them. He stopped riding his bike and acted like he was angry with every costumer who came into his shop. The truth is, over time, you can come to resent any undertaking. But what if your goal was to be fantastic at your job? What if your goal was to be bold in every circumstance?

Second, pray for peace of mind. I've been on many retreats, and it was on one of these special trips that I felt the presence of God guide me toward an answer I'd been seeking. Spiritual retreats often help block the noise and distractions of everyday life and help you gain focus. But God doesn't only speak to us at some camp in the woods or a conference away from work, home, and living. He speaks to us every day! There are moments every day that reveal truth you may need. So every day we must find a way to hear Him. Going for a walk, exercising, or taking a quiet ride in the car can help us relax enough to pray with a clear mind about pressing issues in our lives.

As you start narrowing down your chase, you will need these moments each day. I'm one of those people who spends half my time checking clocks when I know I have a deadline approaching. Why can't we take this same energy and apply it to our time with God?

We can. And we should! Why? Because you have been given this energy to accomplish great things. As you take this a step further, you will begin to realize this God-given energy is perfect for what you were meant to chase.

Third, take action! Don't wait another day. It's time to fly. Be a person of action. Stop thinking yourself into a frenzy and try. Take your dreams, and make them a reality. Write down a plan. Give yourself deadlines. Make your chase believable to the people around you. Make it believable before God. You got this!

VALUE SYSTEM

Our value systems are often created through our environment, education, and experience. Some denominations create bylaws and theologies to help instill some common values, which those who participate can hold to. These can be great, and they can also be taken out of context. We don't want legalism, and we don't want a free-for-all. The idea is to live a life that imitates Christ.

The apostle Paul and Timothy wrote from prison, stating that the greatest value system starts with Jesus. I believe value systems should help create righteousness, not rebellion. This passage in Philippians is an excellent foundation to guide you toward having your own value system.

> If you have any encouragement from being united with Christ,
> if any comfort from his love, if any fellowship with the Spirit,
> if any tenderness and compassion, then make my joy complete
> by being like-minded, having the same love, being one in
> spirit and purpose. Do nothing out of selfish ambition or vain
> conceit, but in humility consider others better than yourselves.
> Each of you should look not only to your own interests but
> also to the interests of others. (Philippians 2:1–4 NIV)

This passage reveals our ability to be a world changer. It doesn't start with our own talents or interests. It starts with Christ, changing our hearts. The Spirit of God purifies our hearts and instills in us powerful purposes.

On many occasions, I've met people who had powerful encounters with the Holy Spirit. One of the first things that change in them is their value system. There's a breathtaking change. The greedy become generous, lust is overthrown by love, slaves are set free, and the helpless become heroes!

95

Before you knew Christ, your value system was based on feelings or cultures. After Christ, it changed; it is based on concrete, biblical truth. We channel our hobbies, passions, and gifts through the Word of God. I have met people who are afraid to do this. They are afraid to lose their creativity and edge. If you truly are trusting God through this process and led by God, your creativity and edge will transform from average to anointed!

BALANCE

The key to balance is defining your core values. Many businesses and ministries are adamant about their core values because they know gray areas within their business models create conflict.

The same is true about our personal lives. You cannot feel balanced if you're living in a gray area. There are times when your opinion may fall into a gray area, but I am talking about your core. You would never say you "kind of love" your wife or your children. It's either you do or you don't. When it comes to relationships, it's important to be clear about your intentions and commitments. Gray areas within a marriage lead to adultery and heartbreak.

Many people have expressed to me how much they love their children and then say, "But I have to make money." Is making money more important than your relationship with your children? You're not a hero to your family if you are making big amounts of money, yet they don't know you.

To have balance, you must learn to stabilize your core values and stick to them. Work is work, and family is family. One of the greatest places to have a hero status is with your family.

There is nothing more rewarding than to feel wanted. Work isn't meant to be an escape from your family. If your family and friends feel it is, that creates room for resentment. Everyone needs to provide for their families, but the same can be said if you're working harder and longer hours to buy superficial stuff. Materialism will surely create an unbalance in how you relate.

When a child first has his or her training wheels taken off, the child often crashes. It's a rite of passage, a valuable reminder that in all things we cannot afford to be off balance. Can't we treat our work and leisure the same way? If we do not focus on maintaining balance … we will crash.

A commitment to balance is a foundational element to boldness. Here are a few rules to help you maintain a balanced lifestyle.

First rule: define your core values. Make it clear to your family and your employer what is important to you. It is important that the company grows. It is important your family members honor each other.

Once you have these established, be ready to remind those around you what your core values are. You might just inspire them to develop their own.

Second rule: power down. I found myself looking forward to having to leave my cell phone on the charger. It meant I didn't have to answer calls or respond to e-mails. I had an excuse not to respond right away. It gave me a break from social media. For a few weeks, I found myself craving this separation. This was a sign that I was spending too much time on my phone, on the computer, and in front of the TV.

People say, "I'm afraid I'm going to miss something." The truth is you are going to miss something, but you'll be gaining something too. You're giving your eyes and brain time to rest. This opens your mind to think under its own creative distinctiveness.

There's so much electronic clutter in our minds. Create a rule that you power down when you're eating with someone. You power down an hour before bed. You only answer texts between certain times. By committing to this rule, you'll create a balance between your actual life and your screen identity.

Third rule: grow in wisdom and stature. This comes right from the life of Jesus. God understands what we need to grow. The balance between wisdom and stature is one of them.

A practical example of this can be found in a passage from Luke, which states, "Jesus grew in wisdom and stature, and in favor with God and man" (Luke 2:52 NIV).

Often, this is true of our adolescent years, but is this true of adults? Some people reach a point where they are satisfied that there is nothing more they need to learn. One morning I was having breakfast with a group of older men. We got to talking about wireless Internet, and one of the men said, "I don't need to know none of that stuff. My daughter figures all that out for me."

Granted, he was in his eighties. I am sure when I am in my eighties, I won't care either about any new technology. But you're not excused from making a lasting difference in this world just because you get older. In fact, the elderly possess a gift others do not: a lifetime of wisdom that could be invaluable to a younger generation.

BELIEVABLE

One evening I learned that one of my mentors had passed away. He was a retired minister who saw his role in the church as one of encouragement for younger pastors. I always looked forward to talking with him. He had a gentle voice and would tell me funny stories from his life that really spoke to whatever situation I was going through.

I had no doubt that he lived an authentic life. I never had to second-guess where I stood with him. He believed in my potential even when I didn't believe in it myself. He reminded me that my calling was from God, not humankind.

Was our bold moment a fluke? Was it a one-time deal? Or are we believable? To be believable, you cannot have any hidden agendas. Hidden agendas make you look like a con artist rather than a world changer.

In order to be a world changer, you need to live a changed life. A changed life only comes from believing in God's will. There is this very challenging passage from the gospel of John that reminds me that until my last day, I am called to share God's love: "For it is my Father's will that all who see his Son and believe in him should have eternal life" (John 6:40 NIV).

To become believable, you must reflect Jesus. Your life, testimony, authenticity, and boldness reveal an undeniable truth to the enthusiasm and joy you display.

DANIEL 11

I've mentioned before that my goal in looking at the book of Daniel is not to take away from the original intent of the text but to look at the boldness displayed by Daniel throughout his experiences and visions.

In Daniel chapter 11, we learn of the rise and fall of men in powerful positions. These kings were right in their own minds. They forced loyalty. They were believable by force, not by example. When these men in authority died, so did their legacies. They could no longer terrorize the land or force their hands. All the wealth they accumulated would, from that point on, be meaningless.

> Daniel states of these kings, "He will be successful until
> the time of wrath is completed" (Daniel 11:36 NIV).

And in another passage, Daniel states, "He will pitch his royal tents between the seas at the beautiful holy mountain. Yet he will come to his end, and no one will help him" (Daniel 11:45 NIV).

These prophetic words reveal that earthly power ends. The common denominator of all these kings is death. A dead man cannot rule you. A dead man cannot give you hope.

Hope fuels boldness. Jesus died on the cross, but He didn't stay dead. He rose from the grave. There were witnesses who saw Him, touched Him, and ate with Him. Without these witnesses, there would be no hope and ultimately, no reason to be bold about our faith.

Jesus didn't leave us simply with His memory. We are left with power. The second chapter of Acts reveals how Peter, who once denied Jesus three times, became one of the voices of Pentecost. The crowd thought he was drunk, but he addressed the crowd with boldness and clarity.

The passage states, "Those who accepted the message were baptized and about three thousand were added to their number that day" (Acts 2:41 NIV).

HERO STATUS: CREDIBILITY

If you are not credible before God, it will never matter how people perceive you. This relationship isn't meant to be something you run from but run *to*. God shapes who you are as a reflection of Christ.

Your credibility provides opportunities for you to be bold. There are many people who claim to be Christians, but their attitudes and actions do not line up. There must be something believable about you.

Let's take a moment to be completely practical. There will be times when you miss the mark. Strangers, friends, and family might see you out of your element. You can even lose your credibility with them. It is a harsh reality. If you're going to move forward, take time to humble yourself before them, and sincerely make a better effort to rebuild your credibility.

You got this! Your credibility will set you up to have a hero status.

Chapter 12

THE BREASTPLATE OF BOLDNESS

Stand firm then, with the belt of truth buckled around your waist,
with the breastplate of righteousness in place, and with your feet
fitted with the readiness that comes from the gospel of peace.
—Ephesians 6:14–15 (NIV)

"I actually feel loved."

There have been situations in my life that I could have avoided if I'd just stayed indoors. If I did what was "safe" or "normal." If I'd only followed the rules or made sure I was being politically correct, I know I could have avoided some situations that would scare some and fascinate others.

In one of those situations, following the rules and doing what was "safe" and "normal" were not considered because I was prompted by the Holy Spirit to do something out of the ordinary.

One night I went for a walk. It was a nice night. Normally I would just walk around the campus, but a friend and I were talking, and I asked him if he wanted to go for a prayer walk downtown. He was always looking for adventure and said, "Sure. When?"

I said, "Right now."

He didn't even really think about it. He just said, "Okay, sure, let's go."

We drove downtown, and I parked my car on the main street.

Then he and I started walking. We didn't have an agenda. I just felt like walking and praying. As we walked, I felt the tug grow stronger. I told my friend that I had a weird feeling. You could say my superhero instincts kicked in. Actually, this was a leading of the Holy Spirit, and we followed it.

We crossed a street and were headed down another block when the doors to a downtown bar opened, and a man started walking toward us. I knew right away. This was the guy.

I told my friend. He looked at me and asked, "What do I say?"

I didn't know either, so the first thing I said was extremely profound. I said, "Hey."

He stopped, lit a cigarette, and said, "Hey. Are you guys out partying too?"

Joking, I said, "Always!" If you know me, you learn very quickly I am very witty. As he took a hit of his cigarette, he smiled and chuckled. I said boldly, "Actually, we go to the Christian college, and I felt like God was leading me to go for a walk down here because somebody needs to know there is a Savior." He looked at me as if to say, *What in the world is going on?* I continued, "I want to share this with you. You aren't alone. God understands your heartbreak." I still don't know why I said "heartbreak." And his response really made me feel stupid.

He looked at me with glassy eyes and said, "Whoa! I've been drinking for a while, but that sounds like a load of garbage."

When I first heard him say that, I almost lost heart. I thought, *He has too much alcohol in his system to care right now.* But that wasn't the case. It was a matter of standing firm and sharing with him the gospel.

I really didn't have to say anything to get him talking. The man continued, "I am sorry for saying what you are doing is garbage. But I'm not normally out at the bars on weeknights, but I found out my wife of ten years has been cheating on me. So I'm out drinking, trying to forget about everything."

The prompting I received was anything but garbage. That night, my friend and I became heroes for this man by sharing the love of God. We spent some time talking. He had a bunch of ideas about God, most of which included *Star Trek* and other science fiction–type shows. But what he was looking for was what we'd come down there to share.

Finally, I asked him if he would ever consider accepting Jesus as Savior. He replied, "No way, man. My life is way too messed up."

I responded with, "Exactly! God is okay with people who are in a jam."

My friend told him what he was in the middle of before he found Jesus. He spoke about his drug addiction, homelessness, involvement with abusive relationships, and his slavery to lust.

The man said, "Holy smokes, bro. Do you want a cigarette?"

My friend laughed and said, "No thanks, but that's the point. You can be a mess and invite Jesus to be part of that. That's the first step."

Then I asked again, "Can we pray for you?"

He said, "Sure, guys. I've already lost everything."

So we began to pray. As we prayed, this man's face became saturated in tears. I could tell his eyes were dripping. And as we finished, he was outright sobbing.

"I thought I'd lost it all, so I went out drinking to make myself feel better. I didn't lose it all because you guys helped me find everything! You guys helped me find Jesus." He used his sleeve to wipe away the tears as he said, "I haven't felt loved in a long time. I actually feel loved!"

CHASE THE FUGITIVE

Our dreams are moments away from becoming fugitives. They can escape when we doubt. They are on the run when we're busy. Your passions and gifts are by no means silly or foolish. They aren't a waste of time if they're fueling you to reach your destiny.

We often allow the fugitive to escape because our hearts aren't ready to endure another failure. Our dreams get lost in talk. We use words like "someday" or "if only" or "what if" as excuses to allow them to become runaways.

So I ask this question of our dreams: Are they still our dreams even when we're experiencing a tough time? Will they be our dreams even if we're in a dark place?

When I played baseball, I had days when I would strike out because I didn't swing the bat. I was waiting for the perfect pitch. Meanwhile, each pitch was a home run passing me by. My father always told me, "If you're going to go down, go down swinging." This really inspired me to start stepping up to the plate.

So often I feel this tension between thinking about doing something and doing something I was thinking about. It's a nagging battle. Until your dreams become actions, they will remain fugitives on the verge of running away.

Are there thoughts that can lead you into trouble? Of course, there are. There's a passage in the book of James that reveals the difference between chasing what's right and chasing what's wrong (James 1:15). The difference between chasing your dreams and chasing after temptation are intentions.

Sexual lust isn't the only thing that can and will get you into trouble. Many times we associate sexual temptations as the end-all of temptations. But there are many more. Some lust for popularity, money, power, and even acceptance.

I might sound like I am telling you to put the brakes on your dreams, but I'm not. The rust and the dust will interfere with your forward motion. I'm encouraging you to seek accountability. Have a person in your life who isn't afraid to cheer for and challenge you.

There are some who struggle with insecurity, and your dreams aren't meant for their ears or hearts. They aren't the right people for you. How can you know who is right for you? How can you protect your heart and still have accountability?

I've had many dreams that I was willing to work for and be coached through. I wanted to be good at sports, so I practiced, accepted advice, and went to camps. If this is true of sports, why can't it be true of your dreams? Are you so unique that nobody can help you? I don't believe this to be true at all. You and your dreams are unique, and it requires time to strengthen them and practice. I can tell you from experience that it can be difficult at times. This does not disqualify you!

You are not disqualified from chasing your dreams just because there are challenges, hang-ups, and even dead ends. Those might be the challenges you need to understand your dream more clearly. These inconveniences are educating you.

If you truly have a desire to change the world, be prepared to chase the fugitive! You got this!

FOUR CHAMBERS

The breastplate, made of metal or wood, was meant to protect your vital organs. Especially your heart. Soldiers knew that if their hearts were punctured, they could no longer fight.

The heart beating correctly decides whether you live or die. Our spiritual and emotional hearts are also under extreme attack. There are words and comments that might seem small but act like bullets. They come in and destroy dreams and ambitions.

I've been in meetings where the one person I wanted to accept my idea responded sarcastically. I left those meetings angry and confused. At times, I could feel my body temperature rise. Digging deep, pressing in, and aiming for the stars are exactly what you need to keep doing despite the opinions of others.

There are four chambers in the heart. The blood is meant to come in and back out. The heart creates pressure for the blood to be passed easily to the rest of the body. When our daughter was born, she had two holes in her heart. She spent a few months in the NICU at the West Chester Children's Medical Center for a combination of problems, this being one of them.

When she was strong enough to come home, there were many therapies. We also had to see the cardiologist on a regular basis. We took her to an office with a *Finding Nemo* theme and an aquarium with fish swimming around. A typical visit included an EKG and the doctor explaining the four chambers of her heart. He drew a four-square diagram and circled the places where her holes were.

God taught us a valuable lesson through this experience. We were a few weeks away from moving and had one last visit with this cardiologist before we immediately started looking for a new one. Our hearts were heavy from all the changes, and finding new doctors seemed impossible.

My wife and I made sure we both attended this appointment, so we would be ready for what came next. We were in a state of grief.

The apostle Paul understood that grief falls on believers and nonbelievers. This wasn't a Christian or non-Christian thing. This was a human thing. Our earthly bodies aren't meant to last forever. But keep in mind our heavenly bodies are eternal.

> Praise be to the God and Father of our Lord Jesus Christ, the Father of compassion and the God of all comfort, who comforts us in all our troubles, so that we can comfort those in any trouble with the comfort we ourselves receive from God. (2 Corinthians 1:3–4 NIV)

CARDIOLOGIST

The nurse doing the EKG and the ultrasound on our daughter's heart was quieter than usual. When she finished the ultrasound, the nurse quickly wiped the gel off our daughter and said the doctor would look over the images.

Within a few moments, she returned and said, "As soon as she is dressed, the doctor would like to see you immediately."

She left without any further explanation. Jen and I were both scared, fearing the worst. So we dressed our daughter quickly and went to see the doctor.

He once again drew the diagram of the heart on the whiteboard in his office. He was grinning from ear to ear as he told us, "I've shown you this diagram many times, and I have to say this. Medically, I'm really not supposed to say this, but I know you're Christians. The holes in her heart closed! God healed her heart!"

We had tears of joy in our eyes. Our fears were gone. Our faith in an all-loving and all-powerful God was greater than ever.

As we put on our seat belts and were leaving the parking lot, Jen looked at me and said, "Really? The holes closed."

I looked over at her and had one simple, small, profound word to respond with: "Really!"

When you transition from fear to faith, there are not a lot of words you can use to truly express the deep confidence you receive. I've never been accused of being a man of few words, but when God moves so profoundly, even I am left speechless.

SPEECHLESS

When we encounter something that is truly more powerful than we could ever imagine, we are left speechless. The massive power of our encounter left us with no words.

There have been a few times in my life when I can say I was completely and utterly speechless. The overwhelming power before me left no ability for me to say anything or give any verbal description at that moment.

The passages from Daniel chapters 10–12 are prophetic messages. God didn't set us up to fail. The prophetic Word of God prepares you for the future. Often these encounters can leave you speechless, and they are vital to your growth.

I jokingly tell others, "I can't heal people, but I often have front-row seats to God's healing power in action." The reality is we cannot separate salvation from healing. Sickness and pain were never parts of the original plan. It doesn't mean you won't get sick. It means you, as a believer, are privileged to claim healing and rebuke sickness. You get to remind sickness and pain of your freedom in Christ. This is exciting because it means sickness and pain never win! This is a benefit and privilege. God is in control and Lord over all that.

There is so much wrong theology that robs you of having this faith. God didn't stop healing. You cannot separate Jesus from healing. This is inseparable! The apostle Paul states in Galatians 3:3 (NIV), "Christ Redeemed us from the curse of the law by becoming the curse for us." Salvation, healing, and blessings are at work in Jesus's ministry and in our lives today. God's power and presence on earth is still here! God isn't creating and coaching us to live like wimps but accept this victory to live bolder than ever as winners!

Before you experience salvation, your status was whatever you could do on your own. If you were good at business, that was your status. If you had a lot of possessions, a terrible status, or made many unrighteousness choices, that is behind you. That is your testimony. From this point on, you have a hero status. You belong to Jesus!

Be a reflection of the ultimate hero who saved you!

A HEALTHY HEART

As the Pharisees attempted to trick Jesus. Jesus was able to see through their plan and quote the scripture. This diffused their trickery. The word of God was simple yet powerful.

Jesus states,

> Love the Lord your God with all your heart and with all
> your soul and with all your mind.' This is the first and
> greatest commandment. And the second is like it: Love
> your neighbor as yourself. (Matthew 27:37–39 NIV)

Stop complicating this! This passage shouldn't be dissected to death. It's meant to be planted in your heart and grown into God's purpose. Let it bring you back to the heart of God. Let this verse bring you back to God in your ugliest defeats and most favored victories. This is your compass to the heart of God.

DANIEL 12

The conclusion of the book of Daniel is exciting. There is motivation from the chapter to hang on to being wise with the Lord. I love the imagery of the shining stars.

The passage states,

> Those who are wise will shine like the brightness of the
> heavens, and those who lead many to righteousness,
> like the stars forever and ever. (Daniel 12:3 NIV)

This last chapter of Daniel is a challenge to him to live diligently until death. You will live your life fully and die, but there is a promise. There is an "allotted inheritance" (Daniel 12:13 NIV). This diligence has a reward. There is a blessing!

HERO STATUS: TAKE HEART

As you look at the threshold before you, get ready! The time to be bold is now. Be encouraged! Do not let another day go by as a victim of the world but as victorious by the word! "Put on the new self, created to be like God in true righteousness and holiness." (Ephesians 4:24 NIV)

Be strong and courageous. Do not be afraid; do
not be discouraged. For the Lord your God will be
with you wherever you go. (Joshua 1:9 NIV)

Now is the time to act!
God has been refining you for this moment!
You are meant to be bolder than ever!
Live powerfully!
Unleash your hero status!

Made in the USA
Lexington, KY
13 January 2018